WESLEY'S
PRAYERS AND PRAISES

WESLEY'S
PRAYERS AND PRAISES

*A selection of little-known hymns by
Charles Wesley, to which have been added
a few by his brother, the whole being
arranged for use mainly in
private devotion*

EDITED BY

J. ALAN KAY

WIPF & STOCK · Eugene, Oregon

Wipf and Stock Publishers
199 W 8th Ave, Suite 3
Eugene, OR 97401

Wesley's Prayers and Praises
By Kay, J. Alan
Copyright©1958 Methodist Publishing - Epworth Press
ISBN 13: 978-1-5326-0478-2
Publication date 8/14/2016
Previously published by Epworth Press, 1958

Every effort has been made to trace the current copyright
owner of this publication but without success. If you have any
information or interest in the copyright, please contact the publishers.

CONTENTS

Introduction   vii

PRAISE AND ADORATION   1

THE CHRISTIAN EXPERIENCE   8

GOD'S SEARCH FOR MAN   8
MAN'S SEARCH FOR GOD   12
FORGIVENESS AND DELIVERANCE FROM SIN   22
THE DIVINE INDWELLING   31
DEDICATION   36
THE LIFE OF FAITH

The daily walk with God   41
Before prayer   43
Before public worship   45
In serving   47
In bearing witness   48
In joy   48
In doubt   49
When baffled by the ways of God   50
In temptation   50
After a relapse into sin   51
After a recovery from sin   52
In weakness of faith   53
In spiritual darkness   54
In spiritual difficulty   57
In suffering   60
In persecution   61

THE CHRISTIAN VIRTUES

The will to please God   63
Attention to the voice of Christ   64
Purity of heart   65
Humility   65
Faith   66
Patience   68

CONTENTS

Meekness	68
Constancy	68
The spirit of peacemaking	70
Universal love	70
Love for brethren	71
Love for enemies	71
Perfection	73
The mind of Christ	75
The image of Christ	76

CONFIDENCE IN GOD

In His goodness	76
In His protection	77
In the abundance of His grace	77
In His forgiveness	78
In His power to destroy sin and create virtue	78
In His power to keep to the end	81
In His victory	82
In His perfecting of the Church	82
In the coming of His Kingdom	83
In His reward	84

THE LIFE OF THE CHURCH

THE SERVICES OF THE CHURCH

At public worship	85
After worship	86
At a fellowship meeting	87
When parted from the fellowship	87
At the baptism of infants	88
At the baptism of an adult	89
At Holy Communion	89
At an Ordination	95
At Conference	95
At a funeral	98

THE CHURCH'S YEAR

Advent	101
Christmas	103
Epiphany	107
Palm Sunday	108
Good Friday	109
Easter Day	112
Ascension Day	114

CONTENTS

Before Whitsunday	117
Whitsunday	117
Trinity Sunday	120
All Saints Day	121

PRAYERS FOR THE CHURCH

For the revival of the Church	122
For members suffering persecution	122
For mutual love	123
For unity	124
For the work of evangelism	129
For the completing of the Church	133
For the perfecting of the Church	134

PRAYERS FOR USE BY SERVANTS OF THE CHURCH

For a chorister	135
For a physician	136
For teachers and leaders	136
For preachers	137
For a candidate for the Ministry	139
For ordinands	139
For ministers	141
For an aged minister	145

THE DAILY ROUND

THE CIRCUMSTANCES OF LIFE

On a birthday	147
In a hurry of business	147
In uncertainty	148
In danger	149
In threat of war	149
In pain	150
In sickness	151
In old age	151
Preparing for death	152

ENMITY

When accused of evil	154
When suffering enmity	154
After strife	158

CONTENTS

FRIENDSHIP

When visiting friends	159
Prayers for sick friends	159
On the death of a friend	161

FAMILY LIFE

Grace before meat	161
Marriage	162
On the birth of a child	163
Parents' prayers for their children	164
Prayer for a sick child	166
A father's evening prayer	167
Prayers for mutual love	167
A parent's confidence in Christ	169
Children's praise	169
A child's prayer	170
A wife's prayer for the conversion of her husband	170
On the death of a member of the family	171

Index of first lines and sources   173

INTRODUCTION

THE MEMORIAL TABLET to Charles Wesley which is set in the wall of Wesley's Chapel, City Road, says: 'As a Christian poet he stood unrivalled; and his hymns will convey instruction and consolation to the faithful in Christ Jesus as long as the English Language is understood.' That prophecy was written at the time of his death in 1788, but the passing of the years has only made it more sure. Since his death no one has written hymns to compare with his in either quality or quantity, nor is there anyone whose work is more frequently used either in the services of the Church or in private devotion.

It was for both these uses that his hymns were written. Even those whose main purpose is to express the worship of a congregation were intended also to be used in private. But there are many others which were written especially for private use—some of them too individual for corporate worship, some hardly practicable for congregational singing because they consist of only a single verse, and some written for his own private prayers. This present selection has been compiled with the expectation that its contents (including those hymns which were obviously mainly intended for corporate use) will be used chiefly in private, and has been arranged so as to be suitable for that purpose.

Much of the best of Charles Wesley's work appears, of course, in the *Methodist Hymn-book*, and since that is easily obtainable, none of the hymns which are to be found there has been reprinted here—except that in one or two instances, in hymns where stanzas are used which have been omitted from the hymn-book, it has been necessary to retain a first or last verse of the hymn as printed there for the sake of making a proper beginning or ending. Not all Wesley's best work, however, is to be found in the hymn-book, and there are hymns in this selection which are as great as any of those in common use.

Wesley, of course, wrote for his own age, but (apart from some points to be mentioned later) his work is singularly apposite for ours. We in the twentieth century, with our concern about mental health, nuclear physics, international relationships, Church unity and racialism, need the message which he proclaims, and we need it expressed in the natural, direct way in which he expresses it.

INTRODUCTION

We need his conception of God. Throughout his hymns there is an all-pervading sense of God's infinite greatness and majesty. They must be called revival hymns, for they were the instruments and products of the greatest revival in history, but they are very different from most compositions which go by that name. A short time ago a little Mission Hall in the north of England invited passers-by to join the congregation in worship by exhibiting a notice which said: 'Drop in and have a little chat with your heavenly Father.' That is the very antithesis of Wesley's way. For him, to worship is not to have 'a little chat'; it is to 'tremble at [His] glory's height, And, lost in silent praise, adore'. He does not think we drop in for it; we come because we have been 'Ordain'd, prepared, disposed, By [God's] preventing grace'. And although he rejoices in the fact that God is indeed our heavenly Father, he believes that His heavenliness is as important as His fatherhood; He is 'The Father shining on His throne', the 'Father of uncreated light', the 'Father of endless majesty'.

He knows God as the God of love, love so 'stupendous' that 'It brought the Saviour from above' and so 'divine' that 'The immortal God hath died for me'. It is true that he sometimes writes as if the Father needs to be persuaded to be gracious, and such hymns are so misleading that they have not been included in the present selection; but even then he holds that the persuading is done by Jesus, and that it was God Himself who sent His Son so that this persuasion might take place. The outstanding characteristic of God's love as seen by Wesley is that it is universal. He never tires of saying that Christ was sent 'for me', but he insists all the time that He was only sent for me because He was sent for all mankind. As against the rigid Calvinism of his day, he insists that God's grace is to 'all', that He is concerned to save 'the world', that His mercy is 'unconfined', His regard 'undistinguishing', and His Son 'The general Saviour of mankind'.

He stresses the fact that God is the God of holiness. His nature is 'spotless sanctity' and He abhors 'the things unclean'. That is why He is not satisfied with anything less than perfection in us; we too must be made holy. There is a difference here between the thought of Charles Wesley and that of his brother. John's stress was on perfect love, which by faith may be attained at a blow, which must be renewed moment by moment, and which (although it is perfect at each stage) must grow as we ourselves grow; but Charles became unsatisfied with this, and his stress came to be on ultimate

INTRODUCTION

perfection of character, a perfection not attained in a moment, but requiring a whole lifetime of striving and growth. Yet there is no real contradiction here; both the brothers were right. We seek after a relative perfection which consists in loving God with all our heart and mind and soul and strength in every moment, and which we can know now; but we also seek to be trained and transformed by God until we reach a perfection of character and thought and deed which it is not possible to reach save by long growth. Although they came to stress different aspects of it, the two brothers were at one in emphasizing man's call to sanctity, and their belief in its necessity was due to their conception of the sanctity of God. Perfection in man is the demand and the gift which is made by one whose own goodness is perfect.

Equally impressive is Charles Wesley's realization of God's energy and power; he sees God as a Being who has 'intense desires' and who 'fulfils' them. The infinity of His power is, as one might expect, seen in creation; His is 'The plastic power that fills the whole, And governs earth, air, sea, and sky'. But it is not God's physical might on which Wesley loves most to dwell; the greatest exercise of His energy and vigour is in the spiritual world, in overcoming sin and creating virtue. God is one who 'confounds' and 'breaks' men, who 'stamps' His image on their breasts, and who in the death of Christ 'pulled the infernal kingdom down' like Samson destroying the temple of Dagon. His Spirit 'breathes the active flame', and the fire of it 'Consumes like flax the cords of sin, And burns up all my foes within'. Because of this power, all things are possible—for the individual, for the Church, and even for the world.

These emphases are supremely valuable in our day. In a generation to which the attitude of reverence does not come easily, it is salutary to be brought face to face with God's majesty. In an age when there are so many who despise a man because he is a negro, or suspect him because he is a Jew, or fear him because he is a Russian, or forget him because he is a refugee, or hate him because he is an enemy, it is good to be reminded that God's love takes no account of such things, and that we can only be sure that He loves us if we are sure that He loves all mankind. In an age when we are troubled not only about murder, prostitution, divorce and physical violence, but about the low level of morality in general, it is good that we should be made to think about God's holiness and His resulting demands upon us. At a time when we are conscious, as perhaps we have never been before, of the strength of the forces

INTRODUCTION

with which we have to deal, not only the physical powers of destruction but the evil will of nations and the hidden primeval energies which rise in every individual, it is well that we should be made to feel God's infinite activity and power.

Equally valuable to us is Charles Wesley's experience of the life of faith. That experience is on the whole a singularly well-balanced one. There is, for instance, a sound balance between quiet acceptance of the work of God and continual vigorous effort. Wesley knew well his own 'utter helplessness' and the fact that God is 'inaccessible' unless He Himself imparts His love. He cannot be pleased without faith, but faith is His creation; He cannot be approached without penitence, but penitence is His gift; He cannot be rightly served without the flame of love, but the fire is kindled by His own Spirit. Everything, indeed, is of God, and therefore the soul must wait for Him—'wait the moving the pool, . . . wait the word that speaks [it] whole'. Yet at the same time, the Christian life, both in its beginning and its continuance, is one of tremendous effort. We are apt to forget what struggles the Wesleys went through before the experience of Whitsuntide 1738 and what continual effort they put into their religion afterwards. To wait for God meant to wait in prayer, in Bible reading, in thought and study, in religious fellowship, in works of mercy, in public worship, in Holy Communion, in tremendous activity; it is significant that the hymn generally acknowledged to be Charles Wesley's greatest is 'Wrestling Jacob'. To live with God afterwards involved equally tremendous effort. Believers were 'by endless conflicts tried', they had to meet the perils of the desert, to scale mountains, 'to wrestle and fight and pray'. Those who would enter the Kingdom of grace must do so 'forcibly', and those who would remain in it must 'force' their passage to the skies.

Charles Wesley's experience points to a similar balance in the realm of feeling, though his thought is not always as sound here as elsewhere. The signs of the Spirit's working are joy and peace, and he is right to stress the importance of feeling in religion. There is no love relationship, either human or divine, without it, and one of the signs of broken fellowship is that the joy and peace depart. Nevertheless there are also other reasons for which they may depart. Not only are our feelings at the mercy of our physical as well as our spiritual health, not only are they affected by weariness of body and mind as well as by weariness of soul, but human life is everywhere one of ebb and flow, and we are not intended to be always in a state

INTRODUCTION

of rapture. There is no doubt that Wesley sometimes over-stresses the importance of feeling; there are some hymns in which he seems to be seeking feeling rather than God, and some in which he seems to suppose that he ought to be feeling exhilarated all the time. Nevertheless he very clearly recognizes that in actual fact this does not happen. The hymns most commonly sung are those in which he is filled with rapture; but it is good to remember that he did not always live in exultation. There are occasions when he says 'Outward comforts have I none, Or sensible delight; Joy is to my soul unknown, My day is turned to night'. One of the most valuable lessons he learned was that this darkness was in him and not in God, and that in all his fluctuations of feeling God was still the same. It is not a little touching to find him 'cheerless', confessing that prayer is 'abhorrent' and praise 'tasteless', and yet in the same hymn saying that God is his portion, his treasure, his life, his happiness, his heaven. He comes to know that in the thick darkness of his soul 'the great Invisible is near', and that the glory of God is present even when it is veiled. When he goes to Communion and is not able to *feel* the streams of living water flow, he learns that he must nevertheless 'Do this' as Jesus has commanded. In such a treatment of feeling he is entirely sound.

A third balance in his religious life is that between its individual and its corporate aspects. Both are strongly represented in his hymns. Their references to the individual have sometimes been criticized by those who forget that this is a characteristic of some of the greatest of the psalms, to say nothing of the *Magnificat* and the *Nunc Dimittis*. It is true that in hymns one can have too much individualism, but there is nothing amiss with writing them in the singular so long as the corporate aspect of the religious life is not neglected. Wesley does not neglect it. He conceives of God as not only the Father of the individual, but the God who 'makes us one'; Jesus is seen as not only the Saviour of every Christian man, but the Head of the Church; and the Spirit is given not only to the individual, but to Christ's mystic Body. When we give ourselves to God, therefore, it is in order not only 'With Thee' but 'With Thee and Thine to live and die'. It is into the Church that we are received in baptism, in the fellowship of the Church that we are built up, with the Church above and below that we sing praise, with the Church that we partake of the Holy Supper, and for the perfecting of the Church as much as the perfecting of the individual that we pray. Often, Wesley deliberately combines the individual and cor-

INTRODUCTION

porate, as when he begins one hymn 'Thou Shepherd of Israel and mine', and ends another 'Drop peace and joy and righteousness On all Thy Church and me'.

These aspects of Wesley's Christian experience are as salutary as the things he stresses about the nature of God, and he expresses them in the kind of way which suits our age. First, as has often been pointed out, he is always biblical, and he therefore speaks with authority to a generation which is learning to take the Bible more seriously than it has been taken for some time. Of course he does not always use it in the best possible way; it is difficult, to imagine anyone singing:

> Forlorn, forsaken, and alone,
> Naked and void of God,
> My feeble soul can scarcely groan
> A dying Ichabod.

But he is always expounding it and speaking its language. He went through the whole Bible from Genesis to Revelation writing hymns on every passage which seemed to him significant; but not only that—all his hymns are full of an extraordinary number of scriptural reminiscences and quotations. Luke Wiseman counted twenty-three in 'O Thou who camest from above', and Henry Bett found six in the first verse of 'Behold the servant of the Lord'. This use of scripture brings extraordinary enrichment to Wesley's verse. He has only to begin a hymn with the line 'O Thou Good Samaritan', and we see ourselves wounded and distressed, realize that Jesus comes to us in our need, and find Him bringing oil and wine for our healing. He has only to say 'Speak to my warring passions: Peace. Say to my trembling heart: Be still', and we conjure up the scene on the lake, and are convinced of Christ's power to still any storm. But more than that—he uses the language and the thought of scripture to express a vivid personal experience, and the result is that the Bible comes alive, and the experience is seen to be that which has been offered to the people of God through all the centuries. The Bible is shown to be dealing with the truth, and Wesley is shown to be but one of those who have experienced it.

Secondly, Wesley is unshakably rooted in holy confidence. He not only believes that with God all good things are possible; he believes that they will come to pass. God has the will to accomplish them, for He is love; He has the power to do what He wills, for He is almighty; and the issue is therefore settled—

INTRODUCTION

> Thou canst o'ercome this heart of mine,
> Thou wilt victorious prove;
> For everlasting strength is Thine
> And everlasting love.

And if that is not enough, he points to the 'signs infallible' in which we can see God working out His purpose, those first fruits of victory which can actually be 'felt and seen'—the gifts of forgiveness and of the fruit of the Spirit. These things may not be known to those who go merely by 'feeble sense' or 'reason's glimmering ray', but those who have faith have 'strong commanding evidence' of them. There is of course more to be said than this, and Wesley admits that 'A gracious soul may fall from grace' and not be recovered, that 'The salt may lose its seasoning power, And never, never find it more', but that is a side of the truth which appears in his work comparatively seldom. For the most part, he loves to dwell upon the complementary truth, that God will never loose His hold on us, and that, in an oft-repeated phrase, He is 'greater than our heart'.

The result is that Wesley believes that God actually will perfect us, that a time is really coming when we 'shall be from sin set free, Perfectly set free from all', and when we 'shall perform His utmost will'. We can exult because 'We are all to infallible victory led'. Not only so, but the Church too will be made perfect. God, he says, 'cannot miss of His design', and therefore His messengers 'His Church shall build, And lead His feeblest people on, Till our souls with God are filled, For ever sanctified'. He does not despair even of the world as a whole, and he looks forward to that day when

> He will the steadfast mind impart,
> The power that never shall remove,
> And fix in every sinless heart
> His throne of everlasting love.

Thirdly, he always writes with tremendous vigour, intensity, and enthusiasm. Those who only half-heartedly want to serve God, and for whom the pleasures of the world seem more real and desirable than those of the spirit, find in him a tremendous revelation of the joy and exaltation to be found in God's service. His feelings are all intense. When united with God, he does not feel pleasure but rapture; when separated from Him, his state is not difficult but desperate; when penitent, he does not merely feel himself to be a sinner

INTRODUCTION

but the chief of sinners—even though the phrase involves him, in hymns intended for corporate worship, in the unreality of inviting each member of the congregation to declare himself a worse sinner than the rest. His intensity is shown, too, in the speed with which he sees everything happen. The grace of God in the heart moves 'swift' to its source; the millennial year 'rushes' on to our view; he 'flies' home 'like a bounding hart'; he expects the fiery chariot to 'whirl' him to the starry crown; and having arrived in heaven he knows he will be 'implunged' in the glorious abyss—not gradually illuminated, but suddenly swept off his feet and flung into glory headlong.

His enthusiasm reveals itself again in the way in which he piles word upon word and idea upon idea. There is the same zest in him as that which made the New Testament writers speak of the breadth and length and height and depth of the love of God, and enumerate the things which cannot separate us from it, and pile one upon another great words of praise. Like them, he loves to add together the dimensions of God's love, to rejoice in the fact that partakers of God's grace 'Nor joy, nor grief, nor time, nor place, Nor life, nor death can part', and to cry out (adding to the already long catalogue in Revelation):

> Then let us adore,
>   And give Him His right,
>   All glory and power,
>   All wisdom and might,
>   All honour and blessing,
>   With angels above,
>   And thanks never-ceasing,
>   And infinite love.

But if he learnt how to do this from the New Testament, he nevertheless developed it in his own way. Sometimes he used a quite short, simple chain of nouns—'Life and happiness and heaven'. Sometimes he is more rich and full—

> Pardon, and power, and joy, and peace,
> And pure delight, and perfect bliss,
> And everlasting love.

But always the device (if it can be so called) springs from an enthusiasm for the untold abundance of God's love.

INTRODUCTION

It is this same enthusiasm which makes him love to dwell on the utmost limits of things and to struggle with ideas which often can only be expressed in negatives. So he describes his faith as impenetrable, his joy as unspeakable, his peace as unutterable, his love as an inextinguishable blaze; and looking to God he sees that His grace is infinite, His goodness unfathomable, His love unsearchable, and his mind unconquerable. Others recognize these divine attributes intellectually; Wesley glories in them and exults without measure. It is not everyone who feels thus strongly, nor does anyone do so at all times, and therefore Wesley does not satisfy us in every spiritual condition. But over and over again he kindles enthusiasm when it is lacking, and at all times he helps us to see the glory and immensity of the things of God.

Fourthly, Wesley has an immense fund of sound, practical common sense. His imagination may fly up to the heavens, but his feet remain firmly planted on the earth; his heart may be on fire, but that does not incapacitate his head; his aim may be the ideal, but his way of reaching it is supremely practical. There is no nonsense about him.

He believes, for instance, that Christians should use the reasoning power which the Spirit gives them, holding that 'none are rational indeed But those that love the Lord'. In the same breath in which he asks for 'a praying heart' he therefore asks for 'an active mind'. He begins one of his hymns about the apostle Paul with the line, 'Reason he did not cast aside'; and when writing about the occasion when Peter was brought out of a dungeon by an angel, and after seeing the brethren fled to 'another place', he says:

> Out of the dungeon brought,
>   Through reason's light alone
> The ambassador of Christ is taught
>   His furious foes to shun;
> The man of prudent zeal
>   Withdraws out of their sight,
> And when preserved by miracle
>   Preserves himself by flight.

His mind was essentially practical. Faith to him was certainly emotional, but it involved action just as surely as feeling; it worked itself out in deeds. He had not time for it unless it was 'practical faith and real love'. He told his fellow-Christians: 'Your faith by holy tempers prove; By actions show your sins forgiven.' The

INTRODUCTION

hymn 'Omnipotent Redeemer', as it is usually sung, contains the lines

> And lo in Thee
> We myriads see
> Of justified believers.

That is sound and orthodox enough, but it is not Wesley's original; what he wrote was 'practical believers'. Practical belief included for him not only those great works which we think of as typical of Christianity, but also such ordinary commonplace virtues as 'sobriety' and 'courtesy'. It involved careful attention to one's ordinary, small, regular duties—

> Their earthly task who fail to do
> Neglect their heavenly business too,
> Nor know what faith and duty mean
> Who use religion as a screen,
> Asunder put what God hath joined—
> A diligent and pious mind.

All this shows itself in his general attitude and style. There is as much common sense about his language as there is rapture. His manner is direct, his constructions are simple, and his words, in general, are easily understood. There is nothing high-flown about his language, and he does not favour what we call poetic words. It is true that he loves a good classicism and the rolling majesty of polysyllables, but these things stand out only because of the contrast they make with the very ordinary words which form most of his vocabulary. It is easy to quote a number of them, but they are nearly all perfectly lucid, and when it is remembered that they are spread over some 7,000 poems, it is easy to see that they do not amount to much. The same thing is true of his metaphors. There is a commonplace, down-to-earth quality about them. Most of them are biblical and nearly all of them are within the experience of the common man. His favourite metaphors, indeed, are literally down-to-earth in the sense that they are concerned with weight and stability. He loves to dwell on the fact that God's mercies are like a 'rock that cannot move', that His grace is 'fixed and permanent and sure', and that His love is 'solid ground'. He delights in the idea of being 'rooted and fixed' in God, 'immovably founded on grace', having 'substantial joy and settled peace' and even 'solid righteous-

INTRODUCTION

ness'. There is a tremendous sense of reality about these very material and weighty ideas.

His speech is that of a plain man—though certainly a well-educated one—but this does not mean that it is without art. A plain man, if he wants to make his speech effective, will use whatever arts are at his command, and those at Wesley's command are very considerable indeed. He employs all the devices of rhetoric and all the known figures of speech. His powers of compression, too, are quite extraordinary. No other hymn-writer could get as much into two lines as

> Power that life Divine imparts,
> Breaks and heals attentive hearts,

or into four lines as

> Ah give Him in our hearts to dwell,
> To fill with life, and love, and peace,
> To constitute, and fix, and seal
> Our present and eternal bliss.

But he uses his skill in words with such natural mastery that it almost passes unnoticed.

It is, I hope, clear that Charles Wesley is a hymn-writer for today. If we need, as I believe we do, one who can reveal God to us, whose experience of the Christian life is a well-balanced one, who talks scripturally with enthusiasm and common sense, and who has mastered the art of expressing effectively what he wants to say, then Wesley is our man. It is nevertheless true that there are some things about him which are stumbling blocks, but in this selection I have tried as far as possible to remove them. Occasionally his doctrine is queer; he has, for example, some odd ideas about suffering, which we object to as much as his brother did, and he was certainly too much in love with death. Some of his hymns, which fitted very well to the circumstances of his own time, do not apply to ours. Some of the words he uses have changed their meaning or tone with the passing of time; we no longer rejoice that Christ 'pompously displays All His glories', nor wait 'the application of Jesus' balmy blood', nor say that God 'smiles peculiarly' on us, nor cry 'Bowels Divine, forbid!' Taste has changed too. Wesley's oft-repeated 'starry crown' seems to us too much like nursery language; 'bleeding Lamb' is apt to suggest a dead carcass rather than the living triumphant figure of the Book of Revelation; the

INTRODUCTION

idea of 'hiding in His wounds' is one which our psychologists have very rightly made us suspect; and although we are not, at any rate when we are at our best, less conscious of our littleness than our forefathers, we do not naturally express it, as they did, by constantly calling ourselves worms.

There is, too, the whole question of the way in which we express our emotions. The eighteenth century seems to have done it very noisily. Wesley 'claps his hands' when he is exulting, 'pants' when he feels strong desire, 'howls and cries' when there is no comfort, 'shouts' when he returns to Zion, and when penitent offers to God 'an hearty groan'. Today we are more restrained. That may be a good thing or a bad one, but it certainly means that these older modes of expression seem to us unnatural.

When we are offering to God our prayers and praises, we do not want, if we can avoid it, to be distracted by thoughts and expressions that seem odd. In compiling this book I have therefore followed the universal example of compilers of hymn-books—that is to say, I have not only omitted verses which appeared to be on a lower plane of inspiration than the rest, but where it seemed necessary I have altered the ones I have chosen. Sometimes, too, I have joined into one hymn verses which did not originally belong together (claiming for this the precedent of the *Methodist Hymn-book*) and have made such changes as this has required. The purists will no doubt shake their heads, but after all Wesley intended his hymns to be used, not merely preserved, and this book is not intended for those who are pursuing historical research but for those who want to pray.

Nevertheless, anyone who makes alterations has to face John Wesley's word in the hymn-book preface written in 1779, where he desires whose who reprint the hymns not to attempt to 'mend them', for, he says, 'they really are not able'. He does, however, go on to say that if they must alter them, they ought to add the true reading. That I have done in the index to first lines and sources.

I hope this selection will make Wesley's hymns more fully known and more widely used, for I am confident that the more we know his work the more we shall value it, and the more we use it the firmer will be our grasp of divine truth, the stronger will be our faith, and the more ready and able we shall be to serve our Lord.

J. A. K.

WESLEY'S
PRAYERS AND PRAISES

Praise and Adoration

Young men and maidens, raise
    Your tuneful voices high;
Old men and children, praise
    The Lord of earth and sky;
Him Three in One, and One in Three,
Extol to all eternity.

The universal King
    Let all the world proclaim;
Let every creature sing
    His attributes and name.
Him Three in One, and One in Three,
Extol to all eternity.

In His great name alone
    All excellencies meet,
Who sits upon the throne,
    And shall for ever sit.
Him Three in One, and One in Three,
Extol to all eternity.

Glory to God belongs;
    Glory to God be given,
Above the noblest songs
    Of all in earth or heaven.
Him Three in One, and One in Three,
Extol to all eternity.

Father of uncreated light,
    Fountain of life and Source of power,
We tremble at Thy glory's height,
    And lost in silent praise adore.

PRAISE AND ADORATION

Truly Thou art a secret God,
  That hid'st Thee in the deepest shade;
Thy inaccessible abode
  Thou hast in cloud and darkness made.

Darkness and cloud surround Thy throne,
  And veil the brightness of Thy face;
Still we revere a God unknown,
  A bottomless abyss of grace.

Who, who can all Thy counsel see,
  Thine uttermost perfection prove,
Fathom the depths of Deity,
  The mystery of redeeming love!

Thy judgments all our thoughts transcend,
  Thy love is written on our heart,
Thy love in part we comprehend,
  Love, only love, we know Thou art.

O God, at Thy command we rise
  Thy glorious name to bless,
Thee the great Lord of earth and skies
  We joyfully confess.

Our joy is now to sing of Thee,
  To triumph in Thy love,
And this (transporting thought!) shall be
  Our endless work above.

Glory to God, and praise, and love
  Be ever, ever given,
By saints below, and saints above,
  The Church in earth and heaven.

Sing we merrily to God,
  We the creatures of His grace;
We, the purchase of His blood,
  Only live to sing and praise.

PRAISE AND ADORATION

Make we then a cheerful noise,
 Every child of Adam joined,
Share the universal joys,
 Shout the Friend of all mankind.

BLEST be our everlasting Lord,
 Our Father, God, and King;
Thy sovereign greatness we record,
 Thy glorious power we sing.
By Thee the victory is given,
 The majesty divine;
And strength, and might, and earth and heaven
 And all therein is Thine.

The kingdom, Lord, is Thine alone,
 Who dost Thy right maintain,
And high on Thine eternal throne
 O'er men and angels reign.
Riches, as seemeth good to Thee,
 Thou dost, and honour give;
And kings their power and dignity
 Out of Thine hand receive.

Thou hast on us the grace bestowed
 Thy greatness to proclaim,
And therefore now we thank our God,
 And praise Thy glorious name;
Thy glorious name and nature's powers
 Thou hast to man made known,
And all the Deity is ours,
 Through Thine incarnate Son.

GLORY, and thanks, and love,
 And everlasting praise
Ascribe to God, who reigns above,
 Supreme in power and grace;

PRAISE AND ADORATION

To His co-equal Son,
The dear-bought sinners' Friend,
Jesus, who freely loves His own,
And loves them to the end;

To God the Comforter,
The earnest and the seal,
The witness of our sonship here,
The gift unspeakable.

To the great triune God
Be ceaseless honours given,
Till Christ, descending in the cloud,
Turns all our earth to heaven.

AMAZING height of love divine!
  With all Thy Church on earth we praise
The unutterably great design,
  The mystery of redeeming grace.

Wisdom, and power, and strength, and might
  Thou, Lord, art worthy to receive;
Honour and riches are Thy right,
  And blessings more than earth can give.

Help us to praise our glorious King,
  Ye Church of the first-born above;
Let angels and archangels sing
  The triumphs of all-conquering love.

Let earth and all her fulness still
  Rejoice His greatness to proclaim,
And everlasting praises fill
  The heaven of heavens with Jesu's name.

PRAISE AND ADORATION

Meet and right it is that all
  Should, in one thanksgiving joined,
On the common Saviour call,
  Praise the Lord of all mankind.

Mighty miracles of love,
  Jesus, Thou for us hast wrought;
Thou, descended from above,
  Hast by blood the nations bought.

Raised, Thou dost Thy members raise,
  Pour Thy Spirit from on high,
Fill the vessels of Thy grace,
  Fit, and bear us to the sky.

What endless scenes of wonder rise
And strike with rapturous surprise
The heavenly host who Jesus see
In all His glorious majesty!

Angels adore the King of kings,
Their faces shadowing with their wings,
And saints the o'erpowering vision prove,
In deepest awe of speechless love.

Thee the angelic armies praise,
  Those first-born sons of light,
But cannot look on Jesu's face
  And bear the dazzling sight;
Ranks upon ranks, they fall before
  The all-abasing Name,
In silent ecstasy to adore
  The glories of the Lamb.

PRAISE AND ADORATION

WHEN Jesus darts His glorious light,
All heaven is ravished with the sight;
The cherubs strike their golden lyres,
The seraphs glow with brighter fires:
But when Jesus shows His face,
All are hushed and lost in praise.

SAVIOUR, the mystery of Thy grace
Shall be the matter of my praise,
That grace which fills the hosts above
With joy, astonishment, and love.

SALVATION to our God
　That sits upon the throne;
Salvation be alike bestowed
　On His triumphant Son.

The Lamb for sinners slain,
　Who died to die no more,
Let all the ransomed sons of men
　With all His hosts adore.

Let earth and heaven be joined
　His glories to display,
And hymn the Saviour of mankind
　In one eternal day.

ALL CREATURES, praise the Eternal Name.
　Ye hosts that to His courts belong,
Cherubic choirs, seraphic flames,
　Awake the everlasting song.
All ye who owe to Him your birth,
　In praise your every hour employ;
Jehovah reigns! Be glad, O earth,
　And shout ye morning stars for joy.

PRAISE AND ADORATION

We, Saviour, at Thy footstool lie,
   Thy creatures purchased by Thy blood,
And 'Holy, holy, holy,' cry,
   In honour of the Triune God;
With angels and archangels join,
   With all the ransomed sons of grace,
Extol the Majesty divine,
   And breathe unutterable praise.

GLORIOUS God, accept a heart
   That longs to sing Thy praise.
Thou without beginning art,
   And without end of days;
Thou, a Spirit invisible,
   Dost to none Thy fulness show;
None Thy majesty can tell,
   Or all Thy Godhead know.

Sovereign, everlasting Lord,
   How excellent Thy name!
Held in being by Thy word,
   Thee all Thy works proclaim.
Through this earth Thy glories shine,
   Through those dazzling worlds above;
All confess the Source divine,
   The almighty God of love.

The Christian Experience

GOD'S SEARCH FOR MAN

AUTHOR of every work divine,
Who dost through both creations shine,
    The God of nature and of grace,
Thy glorious steps in all we see,
And wisdom attribute to Thee,
    And power, and majesty, and praise.

Thou art the Universal Soul,
The plastic power that fills the whole,
    And governs earth, air, sea, and sky;
The creatures all Thy breath receive,
And who by Thy inspiring live,
    Without Thy inspiration die.

Spirit immense, eternal Mind,
Thou on the souls of lost mankind
    Dost with benignest influence move,
Pleased to restore the ruined race,
And new-create a world of grace
    In all the image of Thy love.

STILL on the soul of fallen man
    Thou dost a beam of glory shed,
A ray of grace, a hidden grain,
    A spark of life, a heavenly seed.

He wakes, and thinks, by slow degrees,
    Nor yet the Principle perceives,
Nor knows the Light by which he sees,
    Nor feels the Life by which he lives.

GOD'S SEARCH FOR MAN

Thou goest about in every age,
　Dark, sin-sick souls to teach and heal;
The published word, the written page,
　Conveys the balm infallible.

We now Thy Spirit of love receive,
　Of power, and of a vigorous mind,
And still Thou in Thyself wouldst give
　Life, health, and heaven, to all mankind.

Ancient of Days, why didst Thou come,
And stoop to a poor virgin's womb,
　Contracted to a span?
Flesh of our flesh why wast Thou made,
And humbly in a manger laid,
　The new-born Son of Man?

Love, only love, Thy heart inclined,
And brought Thee, Saviour of mankind,
　Down from Thy throne above;
Love made my God a man of grief,
Distressed Thee sore for my relief.
　Oh mystery of love!

To fill my soul it emptied Thee;
It made Thee poor, that I might be
　Enriched with every grace.
Love made Thee to Thy Father cry,
And hid His face from Thee, that I
　Might always see His face.

Because Thou lovedst and diedst for me,
Cause me, my Jesus, to love Thee,
　And gladly to resign
Whate'er I have, whate'er I am;
My life be all with Thine the same,
　And all Thy death be mine.

THE CHRISTIAN EXPERIENCE

SEE, THE Desire of Nations comes.
No outward pomp bespeaks Him near;
A veil of flesh the God assumes,
A servant's form He stoops to wear.

He lays His every glory by;
Ignobly low, obscurely mean,
Of beauty void, in reason's eye,
The Source of Loveliness is seen.

Rejected and despised of men,
A Man of griefs, inured to woe,
His only intimate is pain,
And grief is all His life below.

Surely for us He humbled was,
And grieved with sorrows not His own;
Of all His woes were we the cause;
We filled His soul with pangs unknown.

And oh, with our transgressions stained,
For our offence He wounded was;
Ours were the sins that bruised and pained
And scourged, and nailed Him to the cross.

But He His numerous seed shall see,
Scattered through all the earth abroad,
Blest with His immortality,
Begot by Him, and born of God.

Head to His Church o'er all below,
Long shall He here His sons sustain;
Their bounding hearts His power shall know,
And bless the loved Messiah's reign.

HE VISITS us unsought,
And freely doth inspire
Our hearts with every serious thought
And every good desire.

GOD'S SEARCH FOR MAN

STUPENDOUS love of God Most High!
He comes to meet us from the sky
   In mildest majesty;
Full of unutterable grace,
He calls the weary burdened race:
   Come all for help to Me.

Mine utter helplessness I feel;
But Thou, who gavest the feeble will,
   The effectual grace supply.
Be Thou my strength, my light, my way,
And bid my soul the call obey,
   And to Thy bosom fly.

Fulfil Thine own intense desire,
And now into my heart inspire
   The power of faith and love;
Then, Saviour, then to Thee I come,
And find on earth the life, the home,
   The rest of saints above.

WHAT depths of wisdom and of grace
   Do we in Jesus find,
Reflecting on His wondrous ways
   And dealings with mankind!
He marks our unavailing pain
   While far from Him we rove,
And carries on the secret plan
   Of His mysterious love.

Saviour, with thankful awe I see
   Thy mercy's strange design,
Which let me swerve awhile from Thee
   To make me always Thine.
To save my soul, Thou cam'st unsought,
   True liberty to give,
And in the arms of mercy caught
   Thy thoughtless fugitive.

THE CHRISTIAN EXPERIENCE

MAN'S SEARCH FOR GOD

FATHER, Thou hast our hearts inclined,
   Or we had never sought Thy Son.
We still Thy powerful drawings find,
   But cannot rest in grace begun;
Come now, Thine own desires fulfil,
And Jesus in our hearts reveal.

For this, O God, Thou hast us wrought,
   That now we might Thy Son confess;
Led by preventing grace and taught,
   That we might be His witnesses.
Command the light of faith to shine,
And self give place to love divine.

O THOU Good Samaritan,
   In Thee is all my hope;
Only Thou canst succour man,
   And raise the fallen up.
Hearken to my dying cry,
My wounds compassionately see,
   Me a sinner pass not by,
   Who cry for help to Thee.

JESU, Thine aid afford,
   If still the same Thou art;
To Thee I look, to Thee, my Lord,
   Lift up a helpless heart.

Thou seest my tortured breast,
   The strugglings of my will,
The foes that interrupt my rest,
   The agonies I feel.

MAN'S SEARCH FOR GOD

I long to see Thy face;
   Thy Spirit I implore,
The living water of Thy grace,
   That I may thirst no more.

Come, and possess me whole,
   Nor hence again remove;
Settle, and fix my wavering soul,
   With all Thy weight of love.

My Life, my Portion Thou;
   Thou all-sufficient art.
My Hope, my heavenly Treasure, now
   Enter, and keep my heart.

How SHALL a sinful man presume
   To enter that most holy place?
A thick impenetrable gloom
   Conceals the brightness of His face,
Darkness and clouds surround His throne,
And hide from man the God unknown.

God inaccessible Thou art;
   Thou must unsearchable remain,
Unless Thy love itself impart
   To soothe Thy fallen creature's pain,
To cheer me with celestial light
And rescue from eternal night.

Send forth a ray of faith divine,
   (Which only can proceed from Thee)
In this dark desperate heart to shine;
   Ah, give me eyes my God to see,
My Father full of pardoning grace,
A smile upon Thy glorious face.

THE CHRISTIAN EXPERIENCE

FAR FROM myself to Thee,
Thou sinners' Friend, I fly,
Forced out by my own misery
To seek salvation nigh;
The infallible relief
Assured at last to prove,
And lose my depths of sin and grief
In Thy abyss of love.

SUN OF righteousness, arise
   My trembling heart to cheer;
Thou whose glory fills the skies,
   Be manifested here.
Banish darkness from my mind;
All my unbelief remove;
   Heal my soul, diseased and blind,
   By heavenly light and love.

FATHER of Jesus Christ, the Just,
   My Friend and Advocate with Thee,
Pity a soul who fain would trust
   In Him who lived and died for me;
For only Thou canst make Him known,
And in my heart reveal Thy Son.

If, drawn by Thine alluring grace,
   My want of living faith I feel,
Show me in Christ Thy smiling face;
   What flesh and blood can ne'er reveal,
Thy co-eternal Son, display,
And turn my darkness into day.

The gift unspeakable impart;
   Command the light of faith to shine,
To shine in my dark drooping heart,
   And fill me with the life Divine.
Now bid the new creation be;
O God, let there be faith in me.

MAN'S SEARCH FOR GOD

Thee without faith I cannot please;
　　Faith without Thee I cannot have.
But Thou hast sent the Prince of peace
　　To seek my wandering soul, and save.
Assure me now my soul is Thine,
And all Thou art in Christ is mine.

SOVEREIGN, universal King,
　　Every faithful soul's desire,
Unto me Thy kingdom bring,
　　Into me Thy Spirit inspire.
From mine inbred foes release;
　　Here erect Thy gracious throne;
King of righteousness and peace,
　　Reign within my heart alone.

MY HEALTH, my light, my life, my crown,
　　My portion and my treasure Thou,
Oh take me, seal me for Thine own;
　　To Thee alone my soul I bow.
Without Thee all is pain; my mind
Repose in nought but Thee can find.

What in Thy love possess I not?
　　My Star by night, my Sun by day,
My Spring of Life when parched with drought,
　　My Wine to cheer, my Bread to stay,
My Strength, my Shield, my safe Abode,
My Robe before the throne of God.

Jesus, Thy killing, quickening power
　　On this proud abject self exert.
Confound, abase me from this hour;
　　Humble, and break this stubborn heart;
And then my Resurrection be,
And live, my heavenly Life, in me.

THE CHRISTIAN EXPERIENCE

WRETCHED in myself, I would
  Come for happiness to Thee,
Find redemption in Thy blood,
  Permanent tranquillity.

Jesus, kind inviting Lord,
  Thou art my substantial Rest.
Help me to believe Thy word;
  Draw me burdened to Thy breast.

Love, excluding sin and fear,
  With Thy precious Self impart;
In Thy garments dyed appear,
  Show Thy wounds and break my heart.

Let Thy dying love constrain
  My obduracy to yield;
Then I find my rest again,
  Then I by Thy wounds am healed.

'Stablished in my Lord, my Peace,
  Triumphs then my meekened soul;
Never shall its triumphs cease
  While eternal ages roll.

NOT IN the strong impetuous wind
Can I my gentle Saviour find;
Not in a hurricane of sound
Which rends the rocks, and shakes the ground;

Not in the heaven-enkindled fire,
The fervours of intense desire;
But I expect Him from above,
In the soft whispering voice of love.

That still, small voice I wait to hear,
Which speaks Him mercifully near,
Covers with guiltless shame the face,
And wraps the soul in silent praise.

MAN'S SEARCH FOR GOD

SINFUL and blind and poor,
And lost without Thy grace,
Thy mercy I implore,
And wait to see Thy face.
Begging I sit by the wayside
And long to know the Crucified.

Jesu, attend my cry;
Thou Son of David, hear;
If now Thou passest by,
Stand still and call me near;
The darkness from my heart remove
And shew me now Thy pardoning love.

FATHER of Lights, from whom proceeds
Whate'er Thy every creature needs,
Whose goodness providently nigh
Feeds the young ravens when they cry,
To Thee I look. My heart prepare;
Suggest, and hearken to my prayer.

Since by Thy light myself I see
Naked, and poor, and void of Thee,
Thine eyes must all my thoughts survey,
Preventing what my lips would say.
Thou seest my wants; for help they call,
And ere I speak Thou know'st them all.

Thou know'st the baseness of my mind,
Wayward, and impotent, and blind;
Thou know'st how unsubdued my will,
Averse to good and prone to ill;
Thou know'st how wide my passions rove,
Nor checked by fear, nor charmed by love.

THE CHRISTIAN EXPERIENCE

Fain would I know as known by Thee,
And feel the indigence I see;
Ah give me, Lord, (I still would say)
A heart to mourn, a heart to pray.
My business this, my only care,
My life, my every breath be prayer.

Father, I want a thankful heart;
I want to taste how good Thou art,
To plunge me in Thy mercy's sea,
And comprehend Thy love to me—
The breadth, and length, and depth, and height
Of Love divinely infinite.

Father, I long my soul to raise
And dwell for ever on Thy praise,
Thy praise with glorious joy to tell
In ecstasy unspeakable,
While the full power of faith I know
And reign triumphant here below.

To-day, while it is called to-day,
　My willing heart I bow;
I harden it no more, but pray
　And look for mercy now.

To-day, before to-morrow come,
　I yield to be renewed
My Saviour's mean, but constant home,
　A temple filled with God.

Now, Saviour, now Thy servant bless,
　Who always ready art,
And fully from this hour possess
　My unopposing heart.

MAN'S SEARCH FOR GOD

But if Thou dost not now come in,
  Then will I wait for Thee,
And trust Thou wilt cast out my sin,
  And fix Thy throne in me.

BEWILDERED, lost, I must stand still;
  Alas, I can no farther go.
Wilt Thou not, Lord, Thyself reveal?
  I want, I wait Thyself to know.

This moment, if Thou ready art
  To make in me Thy humble home,
Break in even now upon my heart;
  My Saviour and salvation, come.

POOR and ignorant and blind,
Hope in Thee, O Lord, I find;
Though Thou dost Thy gifts defer,
Thee I feel in darkness near.
Thou shalt lay Thy hand on me,
Give me eyes Thy love to see,
Faith and peace at once impart,
Cure the blindness of my heart.

Warned of Thy approach I wait,
Dark, but not disconsolate,
Wait, according to Thy word,
For the coming of my Lord.
Thou wilt soon the cloud dispel,
Pardon in my soul reveal;
I shall feel Thy sprinkled blood,
And shall know my Lord, my God.

THE CHRISTIAN EXPERIENCE

WHEN, dearest Lord, when shall it be
That I shall find my all in Thee?
The fulness of Thy promise prove,
The seal of Thine eternal love?

A poor, blind child, I wander here,
If haply I may feel Thee near;
Oh dark, dark, dark (I still must say)
Amidst the blaze of Gospel day.

Lord, I am sick; my sickness cure:
I want; do Thou enrich the poor:
Under Thy mighty hand I stoop;
Oh lift the abject sinner up.

Lord, I am blind; be Thou my sight:
Lord, I am weak; be Thou my might:
A Helper of the helpless be,
And let me find my all in Thee.

FATHER, Son, and Spirit, come,
   And with Thine own abide;
Holy God, to make Thee room,
   Our hearts we open wide;
Thee, and only Thee request,
To every asking sinner given:
   Come, our Life, and Peace, and Rest,
   Our All in earth and heaven.

Born again that Thee we may
   In spirit and truth adore,
Come, and in Thy temples stay,
   And never leave us more.
Thee our faithful souls desire;
Because we know Thee now in part,
   Nothing less can we require
   Than all Thou hast and art.

MAN'S SEARCH FOR GOD

With resigned simplicity
  And patient earnestness,
Thee we seek; not Thine, but Thee
  We languish to possess.
Come, and bring Thy nature in,
  And let Thy love unrivalled reign;
Grace we then, and glory win,
  And all in Jesus gain.

IF MERCIES without end could move
  So base, so hard a heart as mine,
Its whole capacity of love
  Had surely long ago been Thine.
Lord, for Thine endless mercies' sake,
  My stubborn misery relieve,
And to Thyself this moment take
  The heart which I can never give.

COME then to Thy creature, and tell
  The secret I cannot explore;
Thy riches of mercy reveal,
  Thy love's inexhaustible store.

TILL Thou anew my soul create,
  Still may I strive, and watch, and pray,
Humbly and confidently wait,
  And long to see Thy perfect day.

My whole regard still may I place
  On the faint ray of opening light
(The sure prophetic word of grace)
  That glimmers through my nature's night.

THE CHRISTIAN EXPERIENCE

Here let my soul's sure anchor be,
Here let me fix my wishful eyes,
And wait till I exult to see
The Day-star in my heart arise.

My Lord, Thou wilt not long delay;
This inward calm proclaims Thee near.
Sorrow and doubt are fled away;
My Lord shall in my heart appear.

FORGIVENESS AND DELIVERANCE FROM SIN

ALL KINDS and all degrees of sin
Wilt Thou indeed forgive?
Then I, even I may be made clean,
And in Thy presence live.

Lord, I expect Thy promised grace;
And when Thou hast forgiven,
Pardon shall lead to holiness,
And holiness to heaven.

PRINCE and Saviour of mankind,
Giver of repentance true,
Bring my secret sins to mind,
Drag them into open view;
Show me what I dread to know,
To himself the sinner show.

What I cannot hide from Thee
From myself I hide in vain.
Give me, Lord, myself to see;
Break my heart with grief and pain.
Then my guilty load remove;
Then reveal Thy pardoning love.

FORGIVENESS AND DELIVERANCE FROM SIN

OH WHO can of Thy grace despair,
That sees the thief on yonder tree?
If he could find forgiveness there,
Surely forgiveness is for me.

Remember me, O Lord my God;
Thou art into Thy kingdom come;
Sprinkle my conscience with Thy blood,
And take my longing spirit home.

For Thy own sake pronounce the word;
Tell me, in answer to my cries,
'Today thou shalt be with thy Lord,
And find in Me thy paradise.'

JESUS, suffering Son of God,
   Thy nature is to save;
Let me pardon in Thy blood
   And with Thy Spirit have.
Full of mercy as Thou art,
   Grant the pardon I implore,
Peace to keep my faithful heart,
   And power to sin no more.

COME, gracious Lord, Thy counsel tell:
Must sin in me for ever dwell?
Is this the glorious liberty,
The all of grace which is in Thee?

Thy Spirit in my inmost part,
Will He not purify my heart?
A new, and sinless nature bring
Out of this foul, unholy thing?

THE CHRISTIAN EXPERIENCE

Unless I have believed in vain,
Thy blood shall purge my every stain,
Shall sanctify, through faith sincere,
My body, soul and spirit *here*.

Jesus, if such Thy saving name,
Jesus, in every age the same,
Thy welcome, perfect will make known,
And reign within my heart alone.

FROM sin and misery
Come, Lord, and rescue me;
Come my wandering soul to seek;
Come my sin-sick soul to heal.
All my guilty fetters break;
All Thy saving grace reveal.

Still let Thy grace abound
To me a sinner found.
Equal need I always have
To be sought and found by Thee.
Now, and every moment save;
Save through all eternity.

WHEN shall mine eyes behold the Lamb,
The God of my salvation see?
Weary, O Lord, Thou know'st I am;
Yet still I cannot come to Thee.

One deep unto another cries;
My misery, Lord, implores Thy grace.
When wilt Thou hear, and bow the skies?
When shall I see my Jesu's face?

FORGIVENESS AND DELIVERANCE FROM SIN

Rest for my soul I long to find;
  Saviour of all, if mine Thou art,
Give me Thy meek and lowly mind,
  And stamp Thine image on my heart.

Break off the yoke of inbred sin
  And fully set my spirit free;
I cannot rest till pure within,
  Till I am wholly lost in Thee.

Fain would I learn of Thee, my God,
  Thy light and easy burden prove—
The cross all stained with hallowed blood,
  The labour of Thy dying love.

This moment would I take it up,
  And after my dear Master bear,
With Thee ascend to Calvary's top,
  And bow my head and suffer there.

I would; but Thou must give the power,
  My heart from every sin release.
Bring near, bring near the joyful hour,
  And fill me with Thy perfect peace.

Give me Thy life; for Thou my death
  Hast swallowed up in victory,
Quickened me with Thy latest breath
  And died that I might live to Thee.

This, only this, is all my hope,
  And doth my sinking soul sustain.
Thy faithful mercies hold me up;
  My Saviour did not die in vain.

Answer Thy death's design in me:
  The guilt and power of sin remove;
Redeem from all iniquity;
  Renew, and perfect me in love.

THE CHRISTIAN EXPERIENCE

O Son of God, in vain
Wast Thou revealed below,
Unless Thou by Thy Spirit again
Thyself to sinners show.

Answer the blessed end
Of Thy stupendous grace;
And still in mercy condescend
To our distinguished race.

Didst Thou not leave Thy throne
For a mean house of clay,
And put my feeble nature on
To take my sins away?

Come then, Thou very God,
In this accepted hour;
Partaker of my flesh and blood,
Display Thy Spirit's power.

My weaknesses assume,
Who didst the heavens bow;
Be manifest again, and come
To save a sinner now.

Now is salvation's day;
Now is the time of love.
No longer, gracious Lord, delay
Thy coming from above.

The same Thou always art.
Thyself to me make known;
Perform the counsels of Thy heart,
And let Thy will be done.

Jesus, by faith approaching Thee,
And bowed in deep humility,
  Thy Godhead I adore;
Thy pure humanity divine
Can raise this dying soul of mine,
  And perfectly restore.

FORGIVENESS AND DELIVERANCE FROM SIN

Thy virtue, Lord, if Thou exert,
The merits of Thy death impart,
  Though dead in trespasses,
My soul shall suddenly revive
Obedient to Thy touch, and live
  The sinless life of grace.

Lord, I despair myself to heal.
I see my sin, but cannot feel;
I cannot, till Thy Spirit blow,
And bid the obedient waters flow.

'Tis Thine a heart of flesh to give;
Thy gifts I only can receive.
Here then to Thee I all resign;
To draw, redeem, and seal is Thine.

With simple faith, to Thee I call,
My Light, my Life, my Lord, my All.
I wait the moving of the pool;
I wait the word that speaks me whole.

Speak, gracious Lord, my sickness cure,
Make my infected nature pure;
Peace, righteousness, and joy impart,
And pour Thyself into my heart.

Physician of the sin-sick race,
Come with Thy plenitude of grace
  To this poor dying soul;
The oil and wine of grace pour in,
And heal the desperate wounds of sin,
  And make my spirit whole.

THE CHRISTIAN EXPERIENCE

Ah give me, Lord, in Thee to find
The spirit of a healthful mind,
   The kingdom from above.
Thine utmost truth in me reveal;
Mine unbelief and misery heal
   By perfect peace and love.

Thy presence doth my bliss ensure;
Thy presence is my nature's cure;
   The truth, the peace Thou art.
And Thee possessing, I possess
Life, everlasting righteousness,
   Perfection in my heart.

TURN, O Thou good Physician, turn,
   Thou Source of unexhausted love,
Sole Comforter of souls forlorn,
   Who only canst my plague remove;
For lo, I trust Thy gracious power
To touch, to heal me—in this hour.

PRISONER of hope, I wait the hour
   Which shall salvation bring;
When all I am shall own Thy power
   And call my Jesus King.

Thou wilt, I steadfastly believe
   Thou wilt, the captive free,
Freedom, full perfect freedom, give,
   And more than victory.

Though now to every sin inclined,
   I shall be as Thou art;
Lowly as Thine shall be my mind,
   And meek and pure my heart.

FORGIVENESS AND DELIVERANCE FROM SIN

Anger and lust Thou wilt expel,
  And pride, by stronger grace,
They can in me no longer dwell
  When Jesus fills the place.

Thy presence, Lord, the place shall fill,
  My heart shall be Thy throne;
Thy holy, just, and perfect will
  Shall in my flesh be done.

I thank Thee for the future grace,
  And now in hope rejoice,
In confidence to see Thy face
  And always hear Thy voice.

JESUS, in whom the Godhead's rays
  Beam forth with heavenly majesty,
I see Thee full of truth and grace,
  And come for all I want to Thee.

Wrathful, impure, and proud I am,
  Nor constancy, nor strength I have;
But Thou, O Lord, art still the same,
  And hast not lost Thy power to save.

Save me from pride, the plague expel;
  Jesu, Thy humble self impart;
Oh let Thy mind within me dwell;
  Oh give me lowliness of heart.

Enter Thyself, and cast out sin;
  Thy spotless purity bestow;
Touch me, and make the leper clean;
  Wash me, and I am white as snow.

Fury is not in Thee, my God;
  Oh why should it be found in Thine?
Sprinkle me, Saviour, with Thy blood,
  And all Thy gentleness is mine.

THE CHRISTIAN EXPERIENCE

Pour but Thy blood upon the flame,
   Meek, and dispassionate, and mild,
The leopard sinks into a lamb,
   And I become a little child.

OH THAT Thou wouldst the heavens rent,
   In majesty come down,
Stretch out Thine arm omnipotent,
   And seize me for Thine own!

What though I cannot break my chain,
   Or e'er throw off my load?
The things impossible with men
   Are possible to God.

Who, who shall in Thy presence stand
   And match Omnipotence,
Ungrasp the hold of Thy right hand,
   Or pluck the sinner thence?

Sworn to destroy, let earth assail;
   Nearer to save Thou art,
Stronger than all the powers of hell,
   And greater than my heart.

SPIRIT of faith, come down on me,
For where Thou art is liberty;
Thy presence looses all my bands,
And melts the fetters from my hands,
Consumes like flax the cords of sin,
And burns up all my foes within.

JESU, to whose supreme command
   All things in heaven, earth, hell, submit,
Upon me lay Thy mighty hand,
   And self shall sink beneath Thy feet.

FORGIVENESS AND DELIVERANCE FROM SIN

Oh let me by Thy cross abide,
  Thee, only Thee, resolve to know,
The Lamb for sinners crucified,
  A world to save from endless woe.

Lift up and fix my steadfast eye
  On Thee the risen ascended Son,
On Thee my Head, gone up on high,
  Firm on Thine everlasting throne.

Though earth and hell Thy rule oppose,
  Thou dost as King all glorious reign;
Till Satan, sin, and all Thy foes,
  And death, the last of all, be slain.

THE DIVINE INDWELLING

COME, O Thou Prophet, Priest, and King,
  Thou Son of God and man,
Into our souls Thy fulness bring,
  Instruct, atone, and reign.
Holy and pure, as just and wise,
  We would be in Thy might;
Less than Thine all cannot suffice,
  We grasp the infinite.

Our Jesus, Thee, entire and whole,
  With willing heart we take;
Fill ours, and every faithful soul,
  For Thy own mercy's sake;
We wait to know Thine utmost name,
  Thy nature's heavenly powers,
One undivided Christ we claim,
  And all Thou art is ours.

COME, O my Hope, my Life, my Lord,
  And fix in me Thy lasting home.
Be mindful of Thy gracious word;
  Thou with Thy promised Father, come.

THE CHRISTIAN EXPERIENCE

Prepare, and then possess my heart;
    Oh take me, seize me from above.
Thee do I love, for God Thou art;
    Thee do I feel, for God is love.

JESUS, Thou art the Lord most high,
    The praying Spirit Thou art;
Enter, and 'Abba Father' cry
    Incessant in my heart.
Essence of happiness, appear,
    Into my bosom given;
Come and set up Thy kingdom here,
    Thou Joy of earth and heaven.

Jesus, reveal Thy love to me,
    And, on Thy breast reclined,
Matter of thankfulness in Thee
    I every moment find.
Whate'er occurs, Thy hand alone,
    Dividing all my ways,
And bringing good from ill, I own,
    With wonder, love, and praise.

If Thou my constant Saviour art
    And Thee I always know,
The prayerful, joyful, thankful heart
    Thou always dost bestow.
I then my true Perfection boast,
    Resorbed into the sea,
All mixed and swallowed up and lost
    In Thy immensity.

JESUS, plant Thy Spirit in me;
Then the fruit shall show the tree,
Every grace its Author prove,
Rising from the root of love.

THE DIVINE INDWELLING

Joy shall then my heart o'erflow,
Peace which only saints can know,
Peace, the seal of cancelled sin,
Joy, the taste of heaven within.

Gentle then to all, and kind
To the wicked and the blind,
Full of tenderness and care,
I shall every burden bear;

Glad the general servant be,
Serve with strict fidelity,
Life itself for them deny,
Meekly in their service die.

JESUS, Thou say'st I shall receive
　The thing for which I pray;
Then give me, Lord, Thy Spirit give,
　And take my sins away.
That I may never grieve Thee more,
　Thy blessed Self impart,
And stamp in perfect peace and power
　Thine image on my heart.

Why should I smaller gifts request,
　When all I ask is mine?
I covet earnestly the best,
　The plenitude divine.
My swelling heart I open wide
　To admit my heavenly Friend;
Come, Saviour, come in me to abide,
　Till grace in glory end.

Out of mine inmost soul I trust
　All sin shall be destroyed,
While Father, Son, and Holy Ghost
　Fill all the sacred void.

THE CHRISTIAN EXPERIENCE

Thee, the thrice holy God, I need,
And nothing less than Thee;
With infinite desire I plead
For Thy infinity.

As TAUGHT by Thee, O God, I pray:
Take all iniquity away,
Thou utmost Saviour of mankind,
Nor leave the least remains behind.

Then, Jesus, then the good bestow,
Which none but the receivers know:
The constant joy, the perfect peace,
The everlasting righteousness,

The patient, meek, and heavenly mind,
The lowly heart, the will resigned,
The primitive simplicity,
The true eternal life in Thee.

All the good things which now I claim
And ask the Father in Thy name,
The gifts for men received above,
Oh give me more than all in Love.

The gift unspeakable confer,
The Holy Ghost, the Comforter,
With Thee, and with Thy Father one,
God over all, and good alone.

Thou art the thing my soul requires
To fill my infinite desires;
Infinite Good, Thyself impart,
With all Thou hast and all Thou art.

THE DIVINE INDWELLING

THOU promisest Thyself to impart
 To all who ask Thyself of Thee.
Open the fountain in my heart;
 Spring up, O Well of life, in me.
The Root and Principle of grace,
 In me let Thy good Spirit abide;
Renew in perfect holiness,
 And add me to the glorified.

Not like a sudden transient flood,
 But fixed and permanent and sure,
The grace Thou hast on me bestowed
 Deep let it in my soul endure,
Swift to its source celestial move,
 Freely fulfil Thy whole design
With all the activity of love,
 With all the powers of life divine.

HOLY and true and righteous Lord,
 I wait to prove Thy perfect will;
Be mindful of Thy gracious word,
 And stamp me with Thy Spirit's seal.

Thy faithful mercies let me find,
 In which Thou causest me to trust;
Give me a meek and lowly mind,
 And lay my spirit in the dust.

Open my faith's interior eye,
 Display Thy glory from above,
And all I am shall sink and die,
 Lost in astonishment and love.

WHOE'ER by Thy good Spirit are led
 In all the paths of righteousness,
Thy people saved, Thy chosen seed,
 Thy genuine children I confess;
And added to the number, I
With these aspire to live and die.

THE CHRISTIAN EXPERIENCE

Send forth the Spirit of Thy Son,
O God, into my longing heart,
That governed by Thy love alone,
From Thee I never may depart,
But following my celestial Guide,
Be numbered with the glorified.

DEDICATION

EXTENDED on a cursèd tree,
Besmeared with dust, and sweat, and blood,
See there, the King of Glory see;
Sinks and expires the Son of God.

Who, who, my Saviour, this hath done?
Who could Thy sacred body wound?
No guilt Thy spotless heart hath known;
No guile hath in Thy lips been found.

I, I alone have done the deed.
'Tis I Thy sacred flesh have torn;
My sins have caused Thee, Lord, to bleed,
Pointed the nail and fixed the thorn.

The burden, for me to sustain
Too great, on Thee, my Lord, was laid.
To heal me, Thou hast borne my pain;
To bless me, Thou a curse wast made.

Too much to Thee I cannot give,
Too much I cannot do for Thee.
Let all Thy love, and all Thy grief,
Graven on my heart for ever be.

DEDICATION

Most gracious Lord,
Thy kindest word
I joyfully obey,
Hold fast my confidence restored,
And cast my sins away.

In each event,
Thy kind intent
Of love divine I see,
And mixed with joyful thanks present
My humble prayers to Thee.

Then let Thy peace
My heart possess;
By Thy unspotted mind
Preserve in perfect quietness
A soul to Jesus joined.

In spirit one
With Christ Thy Son,
Henceforth His life I live,
Till Jesus claim me for His own,
And to His arms receive.

Thou, my most condescending Lord,
    Hast humbly stooped to ask my love.
'Tis no impracticable word:
    I may, I will obedient prove,
Thy grace accept, Thy power exert,
And serve my God with all my heart.

Full of Thy holy love I rise
    To worship spiritual and true;
On eagle's wings my spirit flies
    Whate'er Thou dost command to do,
To answer all Thy glorious will,
And perfectly Thy law fulfil.

THE CHRISTIAN EXPERIENCE

FLY, sinners, fly to David's Son;
Distressed, indebted, and undone,
    Him for your Captain choose.
Let him your ruined cause maintain;
The worst and most forlorn of men
    He never will refuse.

If such Thou wilt indeed receive,
Captain, to Thee my name I give,
    The poorest outcast I;
And joining now the desperate band,
And subjected to Thy command,
    With Thee I live and die.

THY WILL, O Lord, whate'er I do,
    My principle of action be.
Thy will I would through life pursue,
    Impelled, restrained, and ruled by Thee;
And only think, and speak, and move,
As taught and guided by Thy love.

THOU canst not, Lord, a beggar spurn
    That courts Thy company;
Wherefore I never will return
    From following after Thee.

Resolved, where'er Thou goest, I go,
    In all Thy footsteps tread,
And glad like Thee to want below
    A place to lay my head.

Thy people, by the world ignored,
    I for my people take,
And serve the servants of my Lord
    For their dear Master's sake.

DEDICATION

Determined, after Thee I bear
　My cross to Calvary,
And come Thy bitterest cup to share,
　And with my Saviour die.

If now Thou dwellest in my heart
　And I in Thee abide,
Nor life nor death itself shall part
　Or tear me from Thy side.

JESUS, Thou dost not sue in vain,
　Or ask what I can never give;
Thyself dost place the power in man
　His proffered Saviour to receive,
When knocking at the door Thou art
And crying, 'Son, give Me thy heart.'

Come in, Thou Suppliant divine;
　I hear Thy voice and open now.
Take my poor heart, no longer mine;
　Enter with all Thy fulness Thou;
Take my poor heart ('tis all Thine own)
And never leave Thy humble throne.

TRUE Light of the whole world, appear;
　Answer in us Thy character,
　　Thou uncreated Sun.
Jesus, Thy beams on all are shed
That all may by Thy beams be led
　　To Thy eternal throne.

Lightened by Thy interior ray,
Thee every child of Adam may
　　His unknown God adore;
And following close Thy secret grace,
Emerge into that glorious place
　　Where darkness is no more.

THE CHRISTIAN EXPERIENCE

The universal Light Thou art,
And turned to Thee the darkest heart
  A glimmering spark may find;
Let men reject it or embrace,
Thou offerest all Thy saving grace
  To me and all mankind.

Light of my soul, I follow Thee,
In humble faith on earth to see
  Thy perfect day of love,
And then with all Thy saints in light
To gain the beatific sight
  Which makes our heaven above.

SAVIOUR of all, to Thee we bow,
  And own Thee faithful to Thy word;
We hear Thy voice, and open now
  Our hearts to entertain our Lord.

Come in, come in, Thou heavenly Guest;
  Delight in what Thyself has given.
On Thy own gifts and graces feast,
  And make the contrite heart Thy heaven.

WEARY of all this wordy strife,
  These notions, forms, and modes, and names,
To Thee, the Way, the Truth, the Life,
  Whose love my simple heart inflames,
Divinely taught, at last I fly,
With Thee and Thine to live and die.

Forth from the midst of Babel brought,
  Parties and sects I cast behind;
Enlarged my heart, and free my thought,
  Where'er the latent truth I find,
The latent truth with joy to own,
And bow to Jesu's name alone.

DEDICATION

My brethren, friends, and kinsmen these,
  Who do my heavenly Father's will;
Who aim at perfect holiness
  And all Thy counsels to fulfil,
Athirst to be whate'er Thou art,
And love their God with all their heart.

SAVIOUR, I know Thy gracious will;
Thou waitest for admittance still.
Thy knock, Thy mercy's voice I hear,
And open wide my heart sincere;
I use the power my Lord doth give,
And gladly now Thyself receive.

Nothing have I to offer Thee
But wretchedness and poverty.
If Thou wouldst in Thy servant find
The lowly, meek, and patient mind,
Dispread Thine image o'er my breast;
Then on Thy own perfection feast.

THE LIFE OF FAITH

THE DAILY WALK WITH GOD

MONARCH of all, with lowly fear
To whom heaven's host their voices raise,
Even earth and dust Thy bounties share;
Let earth and dust attempt Thy praise.

Of all Thou the beginning art,
Of all things Thou alone the end.
On Thee still fix my steadfast heart;
To Thee let all my actions tend.

THE CHRISTIAN EXPERIENCE

Thou, Lord, art light; Thy native ray
No shade, no variation knows.
On my dark soul (ye clouds, away)
The brightness of Thy face disclose.

Thou, Lord, art love; from Thee pure love
Flows forth in unexhausted streams.
Let me its quickening influence prove;
Fill my whole heart with sacred flames.

Thou, Lord, art good, and Thou alone.
With eager hope, with warm desire,
Thee may I still my portion own,
To Thee in every thought aspire.

So shall my every power to Thee
In love, thanks, praise incessant rise;
Yea, my whole soul and flesh shall be
One holy, living sacrifice.

Lord God of armies, ceaseless praise
In heaven, Thy throne, to Thee is given.
Here, as in heaven, Thy Name I raise;
For where Thy presence shines is heaven.

STILL let Thy wisdom be my guide,
    Nor take Thy light from me away;
Still with me let Thy grace abide,
    That I from Thee may never stray.
Let Thy word richly in me dwell;
    Thy peace and love my portion be;
My joy to endure and do Thy will,
    Till perfect I am found in Thee.

Arm me with Thy whole armour, Lord,
    Support my weakness with Thy might;
Gird on my thigh Thy conquering sword,
    And shield me in the threatening fight.

THE LIFE OF FAITH

From faith to faith, from grace to grace,
  So in Thy strength shall I go on,
Till heaven and earth flee from Thy face,
  And glory end what grace begun.

S*aviour* of my soul from sin,
Thou my kind preserver be;
'Stablish what Thou didst begin;
Carry on Thy work in me.
All Thy faithful mercies shew;
Hold, and never let me go.

Never let me lose my peace,
Forfeit what Thy goodness gave;
Give it still, and still increase;
Save me, and persist to save.
Seal the grant conferred before;
Give Thy blessing evermore.

BEFORE PRAYER

T*hou*, Lord, hast given the wish to pray,
  The longing wish which now I feel.
But oh I know not what to say;
  I would, but cannot, Lord, reveal
The load my fainting spirits bear,
Or tell Thee all my wants in prayer.

Dost Thou not, Lord, my trouble see,
  My sore, unprofitable pain?
A thousand times I bow the knee,
  Approach Thee with my lips in vain,
Present with lifted hands and eyes,
A heartless, lifeless sacrifice.

THE CHRISTIAN EXPERIENCE

A thousand times o'erwhelmed with woe,
   I groan impatient at Thy stay,
Ready to let the promise go,
   Ready to cast my shield away,
The fruitless labour to forbear,
And fold my arms in sad despair.

Jesu, regard Thy suppliant,
   Thy needy, tempted follower here,
And now supply my desperate want
   And send me down the Comforter,
The spirit of ceaseless prayer impart
And fix Thine Agent in my heart.

O THAT the power were mine,
   To saints and prophets given,
The power of faithful prayer divine,
   Which shuts and opens heaven.
Then would I wrestle on
   And more than conqueror prove,
And bring the hallowing Spirit down
   In showers of purest love.

Thy servant, Lord, prepare
   Thy glory to display;
Remove this unbelieving bar,
   And teach me how to pray.
Author of faith Thou art;
   Help my infirmity,
And put Thy Spirit within my heart
   And pray Thyself in me.

SPIRIT of interceding grace,
   I know not how or what to pray.
Assist my utter helplessness,
   The power into my heart convey;
That God, acknowledging Thy groan,
May answer in my prayers His own.

THE LIFE OF FAITH

JESU, my great High-Priest above,
My Friend before the throne of Love,
If now for me prevails Thy prayer,
If now I find Thee pleading there,
If Thou the secret wish convey
And sweetly prompt my heart to pray,
Hear, and my weak petitions join,
Almighty Advocate, to Thine.

BEFORE PUBLIC WORSHIP

O GOD of my salvation, hear,
And help a sinner to draw near
   With boldness to the throne of grace;
Help me Thy benefits to sing,
And smile upon me as I bring
   My humble sacrifice of praise.

I cannot praise Thee as I would.
But Thou art merciful and good;
   I know Thou never wilt despise
The day of small and feeble things,
But bear me till on eagle's wings
   To all the heights of love I rise.

Already, Lord, I feel Thy power.
Preserved from evil every hour,
   My great Preserver I proclaim.
By faith I every moment stand,
Strangely upheld by Thy right hand,
   And know that Jesus is Thy name.

Come then, and loose my stammering tongue;
Teach me the new, the joyful song,
   And perfect in a babe Thy praise.
I want a thousand lives to employ
In publishing the sounds of joy,
   The gospel of Thy general grace.

THE CHRISTIAN EXPERIENCE

Come Lord; Thy Spirit bids Thee come.
Give me Thyself; make me Thy home;
 Be now the glorious earnest given.
The counsel of Thy grace fulfil;
Thy kingdom come; Thy perfect will
 Be done on earth as 'tis in heaven.

WHETHER the word be preached or read,
 No saving benefit I gain
From empty sounds or letters dead;
 Unprofitable all and vain,
Unless by faith *Thy* word I hear
And see its heavenly character.

Unmixed with faith, the Scripture gives
 No comfort, life, or light to see;
But me in darker darkness leaves,
 Implunged in deeper misery,
O'erwhelmed with nature's sorest ills.
The Spirit saves; the letter kills.

If God enlighten through His word,
 I shall my kind Enlightener bless;
But void and naked of my Lord,
 What are all verbal promises?
Nothing to me; till faith divine
Inspire, inspeak, and make them mine.

Jesus, the appropriating grace
 'Tis Thine on sinners to bestow.
Open mine eyes to see Thy face;
 Open my heart Thyself to know.
And then I through Thy word obtain
Sure, present, and eternal gain.

THE LIFE OF FAITH

I LEAVE my cares and fears below;
Joined with Thy praying Church I go,
    By faith the mount ascend,
In strong desire to Christ draw near,
And wait in humble hope to hear
    The sinner's heavenly Friend.

Open Thy mouth, celestial Lord,
Open my heart to catch the word
    Which still proceeds from Thee;
And let Thy lips, replete with grace,
Drop peace and joy and righteousness
    On all Thy Church and me.

IN SERVING

JESUS, I make Thy brethren mine,
    And serve in love's simplicity,
Till from those gracious lips divine
    I hear 'Ye did it unto Me.'

LORD of souls He truly was
    Who Himself their servant made,
Bore their sorrows on the cross,
    Bowed beneath their load His head,
Them to serve His life resigned,
Died the Ransom of mankind.

And shall I His lot refuse,
    Greater than my Master be?
Master, I Thy portion choose,
    Partner in Thy ministry
Stoop alike to great and small,
Live and die the least of all.

THE CHRISTIAN EXPERIENCE

IN BEARING WITNESS

'Tis not enough for me to know
  The things which God for me hath done;
His works I should to others show,
  And make His mighty wonders known.
I cannot hide them in my heart;
  I must proclaim His power abroad,
His miracles of grace assert,
  And give the glory all to God.

The faith which in my heart I feel
  I humbly with my mouth confess,
That others too His praise may tell,
  My Saviour's witnesses increase,
That all His family beneath
  May magnify, with those above,
The God who saves our souls from death,
  The quickening power of dying Love.

IN JOY

The honour we claim
In Jesus's name
Even now we receive,
And happy in Jesus's presence we live.

In His pardoning peace
We all things possess,
And richly enjoy
A fulness of pleasures that never can cloy.

Not with these eyes of flesh and blood,
Yet lo, we still behold our God
  Replete with truth and grace.
The truth of holiness we see,
The truth of full felicity
  In our Redeemer's face.

THE LIFE OF FAITH

Transformed by the ecstatic sight,
Our souls o'erflow with pure delight,
   And every moment own
The Lord our whole perfection is,
The Lord is our immortal bliss,
   And Christ and heaven are one.

IN DOUBT

My Father, O my Father, hear
   Thy weakest child's imperfect call.
Now as a servant I appear,
   And yet Thou know'st me heir of all.
Oh make me know as I am known.
Speak, Father; am I not Thy son?

Allured by unresisted grace,
   Thy footsteps why did I pursue?
Why did I ever seek Thy face?
   What secret power my spirit drew
After I-knew-not-whom to run?
Speak, Father; am I not Thy son?

From whom have all my blessings flowed?
   Who gave me these enlarged desires?
Who made me restless after God
   And burnt me up with inward fires?
Oh let the Author now be shown:
Speak, Father; am I not Thy son?

Who held my fleeting soul in life
   And turned aside the fatal hour?
Who, when I oft gave o'er the strife,
   Preserved me from the adverse power,
Removed the death I would not shun?
Speak, Father; am I not Thy son?

THE CHRISTIAN EXPERIENCE

When twice ten thousand times I fell,
  Who was it raised the sinner up,
The sinner sinking into hell?
  How came I by this spark of hope?
Who quickened me, a lifeless stone?
Speak, Father; am I not Thy son?

If Thou didst see me in my blood
  And bid the dying sinner live,
If freely I am counted good,
  Oh let me all Thy life receive;
Oh do not leave Thy work undone.
Speak, Father; am I not Thy son?

Was not my Saviour born for me?
  Did He not live to end my strife,
Bear all my sins upon the tree,
  Rise from the dead to be my life?
And are His deeds and Thine not one?
Speak, Father; is not He Thy Son?

WHEN BAFFLED BY THE WAYS OF GOD

Do WHAT Thou wilt; it should be so.
  If now I cannot sound Thy mind,
Thy work I shall hereafter know,
  The meaning of Thy conduct find;
Death shall unwind the baffling maze,
  The impenetrable cloud remove,
And then I'll see that all Thy ways
  Were wisdom, faithfulness, and love.

IN TEMPTATION

HOLY Ghost, with grace inspire
  My heart against my sin;
When I feel the base desire,
  Exert Thy power within.

THE LIFE OF FAITH

Keep me till the conflict's o'er,
That sin's desires I may not do,
Till the kingdom Thou restore
And all my heart renew.

I KNOW the power was Thine
Which did from sin restrain;
And saved so oft by grace divine,
I ask Thy grace again.

From sin withhold me still,
For Jesu's sake alone;
And though inclined to every ill,
I shall consent to none.

O THOU who hast the victory won,
Regard me from Thy Father's throne;
Regard my faith, which is not mine,
My humble confidence divine
That Thou wilt all my foes subdue
And bring me more than conqueror through.

AFTER A RELAPSE INTO SIN

JESUS, the grace re-give
Which I have cast away.
I cannot now, as once, believe;
I cannot, cannot pray.
Speak, and the wither'd hand
Of faith shall be restored,
Exert its power at Thy command
And apprehend its Lord.

THE CHRISTIAN EXPERIENCE

Soon as I find myself forsook,
　The grace again is given.
A sigh will reach Thy heart, a look
　Will bring Thee down from heaven.

Lord, I believe Thy mercy's power
　Shall every obstacle remove,
I trust Thy promise to restore
　In me the kingdom of Thy love.

Jesus, Thy word cannot be vain;
　Truth, power, and love divine Thou art;
And I shall love my God again,
　With all my mind, soul, strength, and heart.

AFTER A RECOVERY FROM SIN

Grant that to Thee my constant mind
　May with an even flame aspire,
Pride in its earliest motions find
　And mark the risings of desire.

Grant that my tender soul may fly
　The first abhorred approach of ill,
Quick as the apple of an eye
　The slightest touch of sin to feel.

Jesu, Shepherd of the sheep,
　Pity my unsettled soul;
Guide, and nourish me, and keep,
　Till Thy love shall make me whole.
Give me, perfect soundness give;
Make me steadfastly believe.

THE LIFE OF FAITH

Jesus, I behold Thee now;
　But my ever roving eye
Loses Thee, I know not how;
　Soon I faint, fall back, and die;
Doubt again my heart assails,
Unbelief again prevails.

I am never at one stay,
　Changing every hour I am,
But Thou art, as yesterday,
　Now, and evermore, the same.
Constancy to me impart;
'Stablish with Thy grace my heart.

Lay Thy weighty cross on me;
　All my unbelief control.
Till the rebel cease to be,
　Keep him down within my soul.
That he never more may move,
Root and ground me fast in love.

Give me faith to hold me up,
　Walking over life's rough sea;
Holy, purifying hope
　Still my soul's sure anchor be.
That I may be always Thine,
Perfect me in love divine.

IN WEAKNESS OF FAITH

O Thou, whose word is life and power,
　Whose word and will and act are one,
Who only canst to health restore
　And fill my soul with strength unknown,

Tell me again that Thou hast healed
　The worst of all the sin-sick race;
Assure me of my pardon sealed;
　Repeat the word of saving grace.

THE CHRISTIAN EXPERIENCE

Continual need of Thee I have,
My faith to give, confirm, increase;
I sink, if Thou forbear to save,
Relapse into my old disease.

IN SPIRITUAL DARKNESS

LET THE world their virtue boast,
   Their works of righteousness;
I, a wretch undone and lost,
   Am freely saved by grace.
Other title I disclaim;
This, only this, is all my plea:
   I the chief of sinners am,
     But Jesus died for me.

Let the stronger sons of God
   Their liberty assert,
Justly glory in the blood
   That made them pure in heart;
I am full of guilt and shame,
My heart as black as hell I see;
   I the chief of sinners am,
     But Jesus died for me.

Happy they whose joys abound
   Like Jordan's swelling stream,
Who their heaven in Christ have found
   And give the praise to Him.
Let them triumph in His name,
Enjoy their full felicity;
   I the chief of sinners am,
     But Jesus died for me.

Blest are they, entirely blest,
   Who can in Him rejoice,
Lean on His beloved breast
   And hear the Bridegroom's voice.

THE LIFE OF FAITH

Meanest follower of the Lamb,
His steps I at a distance see;
I the chief of sinners am,
But Jesus died for me.

Outward comforts have I none,
Or sensible delight;
Joy is to my soul unknown,
My day is turned to night.
But my God is still the same;
No shade of change in Him can be.
I the chief of sinners am,
But Jesus died for me.

Still I see His unfelt grace
Descending from above,
But can neither pray nor praise,
Nor fear my God, nor love.
Yet He suffered to redeem
My soul from all iniquity;
I the chief of sinners am,
But Jesus died for me.

Surely He will lift me up,
For I of Him have need;
I cannot give up my hope,
Though I am cold and dead.
To bring fire on earth He came;
Oh that it now might kindled be!
I the chief of sinners am,
But Jesus died for me.

Jesu, Thou for me hast died,
And Thou in me wilt live;
I shall feel Thy death applied,
I shall Thy life receive.
Yet, when melted in the flame
Of love, this shall be all my plea:
I the chief of sinners am,
But Jesus died for me.

THE CHRISTIAN EXPERIENCE

Ah, my dear Lord, whose changeless love
  To me nor earth nor hell can part,
When shall my feet forget to rove?
  Ah what shall fix this faithless heart?

Why do these cares my soul divide,
  If Thou indeed hast set me free?
Why am I thus, if God hath died,
  If God hath died to purchase me?

Around me clouds of darkness roll;
  In deepest night I still walk on;
Heavily moves my fainting soul;
  My comfort and my God are gone.

Cheerless and all forlorn I droop;
  In vain I lift my weary eye;
No gleam of light, no ray of hope,
  Appears throughout the darkened sky.

My feeble knees I bend again;
  My drooping hands again I rear.
Vain is the task, the effort vain;
  My heart abhors the irksome prayer.

Oft with Thy saints my voice I raise
  And seem to join the tasteless song;
Faintly ascends the imperfect praise,
  Or dies upon my thoughtless tongue.

Cold, weary, languid, heartless, dead,
  To Thy dread courts I oft repair;
By conscience dragged or custom led
  I come, nor know that God is there.

Nigh with my lips to Thee I draw,
  Unconscious at Thy altar found;
Far off my heart, nor touched with awe,
  Nor moved—though angels tremble round.

THE LIFE OF FAITH

In all I do, myself I feel,
   And groan beneath the wonted load,
Still unrenewed and carnal still,
   Naked of Christ and void of God.

O Love, Thy sovereign aid impart,
   And guard the gifts Thyself hast given;
My portion Thou, my treasure art,
   And life, and happiness, and heaven.

DARKNESS and clouds around me roll,
   But God shall in the clouds appear;
In this thick darkness of my soul
   The great Invisible is near.
He now in His pavilion dwells;
   And when He doth the veil remove,
And when His glory He reveals,
   My fear shall all be lost in love.

IN SPIRITUAL DIFFICULTY

THE WORK of faith with heaven begun,
   With Christ discovered from above,
By just degrees is carried on,
   By patient hope, and labouring love,
Nor ends the moment it begins,
Nor glory in an instant wins.

That patience of unwearied hope
   Fond nature would escape in vain,
To full-grown grace at once spring up,
   Perfection in a moment gain,
Evade the fight, yet take the spoil,
The sweets of love, without the toil.

THE CHRISTIAN EXPERIENCE

But in Thy life, O Son of Man,
  A way more excellent we see,
And labouring hard through grief and pain,
  Through toils and deaths we follow Thee,
Fight on, while day by day renewed,
And strive, resisting unto blood.

We work till Thou pronounce, 'Well done,'
  The incessant toils of love repeat,
And suffer till our course is run,
  Till patience hath its work complete,
And faith its glorious end receives,
And love alone for ever lives.

WITNESS, thou righteous man,
  If now redeemed from sin,
What agony and pain
  It cost to enter in.
For thou didst knock, and call, and wait,
And long besiege the sacred gate.

The heavenly way to find
  Thou hadst to seek and strive,
And cast thyself behind,
  And rather die than live.
Thou long didst toil and suffer on
Before thou mad'st the pearl thine own.

And when thy old self was
  With Jesus crucified,
Expiring on the cross,
  What frequent deaths he died,
And feigned himself entirely slain,
Yet soon revived, and fought again!

By endless conflicts tried,
  Thy patience seemed to fail,
Thy weary steps to slide,
  And sin and hell prevail;
The tempter thrust at thee so sore,
So near each moment to devour.

THE LIFE OF FAITH

Now in the wilderness,
   Now in the garden pained,
Thy Lord's extreme distress
   How oft hast thou sustained!
How oft perspired His bloody sweat,
And fainted at the Saviour's feet!

Down to the gates of hell,
   Times without number brought,
Thy spirit, as it fell,
   In mercy's arms He caught,
And after countless falls restored,
And showed Himself thy God and Lord.

Thy trials yet behind
   Only to Him are known;
But when thy soul is joined
   To saints around the throne,
Thy soul shall sink with theirs above,
Lost in astonishment and love.

REST to my soul I long to find
In Jesu's meek and lowly mind,
In holy joy and spotless love,
That foretaste of the rest above.
But ah, my flesh doth oft complain,
Tired with the long laborious pain,
And fainting in the vehement strife
I quit my hold of endless life.

Jesus, Thy feeble servant fill
With power to labour up the hill,
With zeal toward the high prize to press,
With violent faith the crown to seize.
By Thee stirred up, I'll strive again,
I'll after full perfection strain,
Instant in prayer's strong agony,
Till pure in heart Thy face I see.

THE CHRISTIAN EXPERIENCE

Then, then my soul with rapid speed
Shall labour up to grasp its Head;
All vigour, all activity,
I live, not I but Christ in me.
Passive, yet swift as light I fly,
Fill'd with the Power that fills the sky,
And draws me to that glorious throne,
To live with God for ever one.

IN SUFFERING

A FOLLOWER of Thy patient Son,
  I would the bitter cup decline.
Yet let Thy sovereign will be done,
  My own I patiently resign,
And calmly rest, whate'er I feel,
Assured Thou art my Father still.

The sufferings which the body bears
  Are still the sufferings of the Head,
And every true disciple shares
  The cross on which his Saviour bled;
The members all His cup partake,
And daily die for Jesu's sake.

Whate'er the members must endure,
  Content, with Him I undergo,
Not grace or pardon to procure,
  But Jesu's patient mind to show,
And all His saving virtue prove
Through sufferings perfected in love.

Wherefore on Him I fix my eyes,
  And wait the counsels of Thy will,
Assured that all in earth and skies
  Shall only Thy design fulfil,
To Thine eternal glory tend,
And in my full salvation end.

THE LIFE OF FAITH

IN PERSECUTION

If Thou preserve our souls in peace,
  Our brethren shall afflict in vain;
Most patient, when they most oppress,
  We all their cruel wrongs sustain,
And strengthened by Thy meekening power,
The more they hate, we love the more.

Our sufferings shall advance Thy cause
  And blunt the persecutor's sword,
Dispread the victory of Thy cross
  And glorify our conquering Lord.
Evil shall work for Sion's good;
Its seed is still the martyrs' blood.

Hail, holy martyrs, glorious names,
  Who nobly here for Jesus stood,
Rejoiced, and clapped your hands in flames,
  And dared to seal the truth with blood!

Strong in the Lord, divinely strong,
  Tortures and death ye here defied;
Demons and men, a gazing throng,
  Ye braved, and more than conquering died.

Finished your course and fought your fight,
  Hence did your mounting souls aspire;
Starting from flesh, they took their flight,
  Borne upward on a car of fire.

Where earth and hell no more molest,
  Ye now have joined the heavenly host,
Entered into your Father's rest
  And found the life which here ye lost.

THE CHRISTIAN EXPERIENCE

Father, if now Thy breath revives
   In us the pure, primeval flame,
Thy power, which animates our lives,
   Can make us in our deaths the same;

Can out of weakness make us strong,
   Arming as in the ancient days,
Loosing the stammering infant's tongue,
   And perfecting in babes Thy praise.

Steadfast we then shall stand, and sure
   Thy everlasting truth to prove,
In faith's plerophory secure,
   In all the omnipotence of love.

Come, holy, holy, holy Lord,
   The Father, Son, and Spirit, come.
Be mindful of Thy changeless word,
   And make the faithful soul Thy home.

Arm of the Lord, awake, awake.
   In us Thy glorious Self reveal;
Let us Thy sevenfold gifts partake;
   Let us Thy mighty working feel.

Near us, assisting Jesu, stand;
   Give us the opening heaven to see,
Thee to behold at God's right hand
   And yield our parting souls to Thee.

My Father, O my Father, hear,
   And send the fiery chariot down;
Let Israel's flaming steeds appear,
   And whirl us to the heavenly crown.

We, we would die for Jesus too.
   Through tortures, fires, and seas of blood,
All, all triumphantly break through,
   And plunge into the depths of God.

THE LIFE OF FAITH

Lamb of God, we follow Thee,
Willing as Thou art to be,
Joyful in Thy steps to go,
Suffering for Thy sake below,

Taking up our daily cross,
Called to shame and pain and loss,
Well contented to sustain
All the rage of cruel men.

Who Thy lovely pattern knows
Cannot force with force oppose;
They that to Thy fold belong
Dare not render wrong for wrong.

Jesu, in Thy gracious power,
Lo, we meet the fiery hour,
Calm, dispassionate, resigned,
Armed with all Thy patient mind.

Suffering here, we threaten not,
Innocent in word and thought,
Harmless as a wounded dove,
Hatred we repay with love.

Turn, almighty as Thou art,
Turn our persecutors' heart,
Let them to our faith be given,
Let us meet our foes in heaven.

THE CHRISTIAN VIRTUES

THE WILL TO PLEASE GOD

Lord, that I may the doctrine know,
A will to do Thy will bestow,
   A humble ready mind
To follow truth where'er it leads;
And then the light from Thee proceeds,
   And then my God I find.

THE CHRISTIAN EXPERIENCE

My simple childlike heart inspire
With fervour of intense desire
    Thee, only Thee, to please;
And make Thy great salvation known,
And bring Thy docile follower on
    To perfect holiness.

THE table of my heart prepare,
    (Such power belongs to Thee alone)
And write, O God, Thy precepts there,
    To show Thou still canst write in stone;
So shall my pure obedience prove
All things are possible to love.

ATTENTION TO THE VOICE OF CHRIST

HAPPY the men who Jesus know,
Who humbly walk with God below,
    His secret voice attend;
From all tumultuous passion free,
Their Guide invisible they see,
    And commune with their Friend.

Oh that I thus on Christ reclined,
His quiet, meek, and even mind
    May with Himself possess;
I want the faith which works by hope,
Which calmly to its Lord looks up,
    And waits for perfect peace.

Jesus, on me the power bestow
To work, or rest, stand still, or go,
    As Thy design I see;
Redeemed from nature's hurrying strife,
I would not take one step in life
    Without a beck from Thee.

THE CHRISTIAN VIRTUES

PURITY OF HEART

JESUS, the crowning grace impart,
Bless me with purity of heart;
That now beholding Thee,
I soon may view Thine open face,
On all Thy dazzling beauties gaze,
And God for ever see.

HUMILITY

LOVELY, meek, and gentle Lamb,
    Pattern of humility,
Called by Thy own name I am;
    Fain I would resemble Thee.

But the strength of inbred sin
    Who can thoroughly subdue?
From a creature all unclean
    Who can bring a creature new?

Jesu, Lord, all power is Thine,
    Nothing is too hard for Thee;
Greater than this heart of mine,
    Surely Thou canst humble me.

Cast me down and keep me poor,
    All my weak supports remove,
Lay the deep foundation sure,
    Humble me by faith and love.

Then in Thy meek, gentle mind,
    In Thy lowliness of heart,
Rest mine inmost soul shall find,
    Rest that never can depart.

THE CHRISTIAN EXPERIENCE

His ARM the almighty Father bared
When God in Christ Himself declared
   Our Saviour from above;
Deliverer of a sinful race,
He showed the world in Jesu's face
   His utmost power of love.

The mystery of Jehovah's birth
Confounds us creatures of the earth,
   Of sin and misery proud;
It scatters every lofty thought,
And man is humbled into nought
   Before an emptied God.

The meek humility divine
Shall heal this pride-sick soul of mine,
   This plague incurable.
Now, Jesus, now Thy power exert,
And with Thy lowliness of heart
   In mine for ever dwell.

FAITH

Oh may I tempt my God no more,
   Nor wantonly demand
Unneeded tokens of Thy power
   And Thy protecting hand;
But humbly safe in all my ways
   On Thee my Lord attend,
And through the channels of Thy grace
   Expect the promised end.

No powers extraordinary I claim
   To help in time of need,
Assured I in Thy favour am,
   And by Thy Spirit led.
A child of Providence divine,
   Thy constant care I prove,
Nor ask a miracle or sign
   To show that God is love.

THE CHRISTIAN VIRTUES

That steadfast faith divine,
Jesus, on me bestow,
To assure this trembling heart of mine
Thou wilt not let me go;
That in all time of need
Thou wilt my soul defend,
And save from every evil deed
Till all my conflicts end.

With me, most gracious Lord,
In my temptation stay,
And by Thy comfortable word
Preserve unto that day,
When Thou, our King, shalt come
With all Thine angels down,
And take Thy suffering servants home,
And with Thy glory crown.

That mighty faith on me bestow
 Which cannot ask in vain,
Which holds, and will not let Thee go,
 Till I my suit obtain;
Till Thou into my soul inspire
 The perfect love unknown,
And tell mine infinite desire,
 'Whate'er thou wilt, be done.'

Oh let me of Thy strength take hold,
 Thine utmost promises embrace,
The Finisher of faith behold,
 The God of all-victorious grace.

The grace I every moment want,
 The fresh supplies of faith and love,
God of exhaustless mercy, grant,
 In answer to my Friend above.

THE CHRISTIAN EXPERIENCE

PATIENCE

Come, O Thou greater than our heart,
And make Thy faithful mercies known;
The mind which was in Thee impart,
Thy constant mind in us be shown.

From anger set our spirits free;
It worketh not Thy righteousness.
In patience let us wait on Thee,
And quietly our souls possess.

MEEKNESS

Jesus, Son of God and man,
   Thy Person from the skies
Turns the wrongs Thou dost sustain
   Into a sacrifice.
Thus Thou dost the pattern show
Of patient meek humility,
   Fountain of all grace below
   For all Thy Church and me.

Very God I Thee confess,
   In Thy oblation join,
   Imitate the lowliness
   And patient love divine.
Virtue from the Fountain-head
And grace for grace I still receive,
   Crucified with Thee and dead,
   With Thee for ever live.

CONSTANCY

Jesu, shall I never be
Firmly grounded upon Thee?
Steadfastly behold Thy face,
'Stablished with abiding grace?

THE CHRISTIAN VIRTUES

Oh how wavering is my mind,
Tossed about with every wind!
Oh how quickly doth my heart
From my living God depart!

Easily I fall away,
Never am I at one stay;
Strong in faith I seem this hour,
Stripped the next of all my power.

Seek, oh seek me, Lord, again;
Let not all Thy gifts be vain;
Comfort to my soul restore;
Come, and never leave me more.

AUTHOR of my faith, I look
  For stronger faith to Thee;
Bless me, Thou eternal Rock,
  With Thy stability.
Steadfast and unmovable,
I then shall in Thy love remain,
Never faint, and never fail,
  And never sin again.

PLANT in me Thy constant mind,
To Thy cross my spirit bind;
That I may no longer rove,
Ground and 'stablish me in love.

Perfect what Thou hast begun;
And when all my work is done,
And when all my griefs are past,
Glorify my soul at last.

THE CHRISTIAN EXPERIENCE

THE SPIRIT OF PEACEMAKING

LORD, give me that pacific mind
Which spreads Thy peace throughout mankind
   And knits them all in one;
So shall He own me for His child,
Who all through Thee hath reconciled,
   And take me to His throne.

UNIVERSAL LOVE

FATHER, if mine in Christ Thou art,
Into Thy love direct my heart,
   And plant in me the mind
Which in my patient Saviour was
When, meekly suffering on the cross,
   He purchased all mankind.

Fain would I the compassion prove,
The strength of persevering love,
   Which nailed Him to the tree;
Then should I every soul embrace,
And feel for all the sin-sick race
   As Jesus felt for me.

That sea of love in me be found,
Without a bottom or a bound,
   That sea which Jesus is;
And let me lose my raptured soul,
Long as eternal ages roll,
   In the divine Abyss.

How MAY we resemble God,
   His genuine children prove?
Jesus, Thou the way hast showed
   In universal love.

THE CHRISTIAN VIRTUES

Let Thy love implanted be,
Pure, impartial, unconfined;
Then mankind in us shall see
The Father of mankind.

FATHER, Thy boundless love we find
Embracing our whole ransomed kind.
Thy love to all Thy works extends;
Thy tender mercy never ends;
Thy kindness no distinction knows
Of bad or good, of friends or foes.

Oh may I Thee my pattern make,
Thy nature, mind, and Spirit partake,
And all the ransomed souls that live
Alike into my heart receive,
By indiscriminating love
My second birth and sonship prove.

LOVE FOR BRETHREN

JESUS, that new command of Thine
　I hunger to obey;
The zeal of charity divine
　Into my heart convey,
That in and for my God alone
　I may embrace, esteem,
And after Thee my life lay down
　The brethren to redeem.

LOVE FOR ENEMIES

IF THOU the power of faith impart,
Lord, I can all things do,
And love my foes with all my heart,
When Thou hast made it new.

THE CHRISTIAN EXPERIENCE

Come, then, with all Thy wounds confessed
  My Saviour from above,
And pour into my vanquished breast
  Thy strong forgiving love.

Then when I feel Thy Spirit mine,
  The mighty change I know,
I can like Thee my life resign
  To save my deadliest foe.

LORD, may I put Thy nature on,
Who hatred didst by love dethrone,
Didst make Thy murderers Thy care
And save them through Thy dying prayer.
Oh may I now Thy pity find
For sinners ignorant and blind,
Endure their contradiction still,
And strive with good to o'ercome their ill.

Patient to all that I may be,
Thy Spirit, Lord, implant in me,
Thy lowly gentleness of mind,
Thy love for all the sin-sick kind.
Then shall I bear whoe'er oppose,
Or brethren false or open foes;
The kiss, the scoff, the wounds receive,
And die myself that they may live.

I come by Thy meek Spirit led,
Jesus, in all Thy steps to tread;
I come, if Thou my heart prepare,
The universal load to bear,
My life for every soul to expend,
And bleed and suffer to the end,
The sharer of Thy passion prove,
And conquer all by patient love.

THE CHRISTIAN VIRTUES

VANQUISHED by injurious ill
    That we may never be,
Jesus, let Thy followers feel
    The love which is in Thee,
Love that turned the other cheek,
Love that earth and hell o'ercame,
    Love unconquerably meek,
    Eternally the same.

Arm us with Thy patient mind
    Which pride and wrath controls,
Then the foe shall never find
    A way to afflict our souls.
Then to sin we shall not yield,
But evil overcome with good,
    Keep the faith, and win the field,
    Resisting unto blood.

Now to every saint, and me,
    That perfect good impart;
Thus we gain the victory
    By the meek, loving heart.
Thus we bear the oppressers down
Till vanquished at Thy feet they fall,
    Forced the omnipotence to own
    Of Love that died for all.

PERFECTION

COME let us arise
And aim at the prize,
The hope of our calling on this side the skies.
By works let us show
That Jesus we know,
While steadily on to perfection we go.

THE CHRISTIAN EXPERIENCE

We dare not believe
That God can deceive,
And never intend what He promised to give.
He hath said, From all sin
Ye here shall be clean,
All holy, all pure, and all glorious within.

Then let us not stop,
But continue in hope
Rejoicing, till all in His image wake up,
His purity share,
His character bear,
And the truth of His hallowing promise declare.

JESUS, life of the believer,
　　Full of truth and full of grace,
Gift of God, Thyself the giver,
　　Fill us with Thy righteousness.

This the fruit of Thy great passion,
　　Peace, inviolable peace,
Present, uttermost salvation,
　　Love, and finished holiness.

THIS is His good and perfect will,
　　That we on earth should holy be,
The fulness of His Spirit feel,
　　And live from sin for ever free.

He wills us long in grace to grow,
　　He bids us step by step proceed,
And onward to perfection go,
　　Till made in all things like our Head.

THE CHRISTIAN VIRTUES

THE MIND OF CHRIST

Plant, and root, and fix in me
All the mind that was in Thee.
Settled peace I then shall find;
Jesu's is a quiet mind.

Then the accursed lust of praise
Shall in me no more have place;
Pride no more my soul shall bind;
Jesu's is a humble mind.

I shall suffer and fulfil
All my Father's gracious will,
Be in all alike resign'd;
Jesu's is a patient mind.

When 'tis deeply rooted here,
Perfect love shall cast out fear.
Fear doth servile spirits bind;
Jesu's is a noble mind.

When I feel it fixed within
I shall triumph over sin.
How should sin an entrance find?
Jesu's is a spotless mind.

I shall nothing know beside
Jesus and Him crucified.
I shall all to Him be joined;
Jesu's is a loving mind.

I shall fully be restored
To the image of my Lord,
Witnessing to all mankind
Jesu's is a perfect mind.

OH MAY I, like Jesus, be
Foe to guile and secrecy,
Walk as always in His sight,
Free and open as the light.

THE CHRISTIAN EXPERIENCE

Jesus, Lord, to me impart
The true nobleness of heart,
The unfeigned simplicity,
The pure mind which was in Thee.

THE IMAGE OF CHRIST

GRANT my importunate request;
   It is not my desire, but Thine:
Since Thou wouldst have the sinner blest,
   Now let me in Thine image shine;
And grant me, in Thy likeness made,
Blameless in all Thy paths to tread.

Fully Thy quickening Spirit impart,
   Thou who hast all my sins forgiven.
Oh form Thyself within my heart,
   Seal of Thy love, and Pledge of heaven.
For ever be Thy name impressed
Both on my hand and on my breast.

CONFIDENCE IN GOD

IN HIS GOODNESS

IN RAPTURE lost, on Thee I gaze,
Full of unutterable grace,
Jesus, whate'er Thou art is mine,
Fountain of excellence divine.
All goodness is comprised in Thee,
Good in Thyself, and good to me.

Thy nature doth itself impart
To every humble longing heart;
And all that after Thee aspire
Shall gain, with Thee, their whole desire,
United to their Source above,
Lost in a boundless sea of love.

CONFIDENCE IN GOD

IN HIS PROTECTION

No, LORD, it cannot shortened be,
   That hand which did Thy servants bless,
Which brought Thy people through the sea,
   Which led them o'er the wilderness,
Which hath to us so often given
Drink from the rock, and bread from heaven.

That hand hath opened wide mine eyes;
   That hand, which now by faith I see,
Measures the floods and spans the skies
   And grasps the winds—and covers me.
It brings the blind through ways unknown;
It holds, it lifts me to a throne.

Kept by that hand, I cannot fear
   Lest earth or hell should pluck me thence;
I trample on temptation near,
   Supported by Omnipotence,
Possessed of boundless power divine,
Of boundless love, for Christ is mine.

IN THE ABUNDANCE OF HIS GRACE

STRAITENED in God we cannot be;
   No bounds His power and bounty know;
His grace is an exhaustless sea,
   Which flows, and shall for ever flow.

All in ourselves the straitness lies;
   Our faith, and not His promise, fails;
He blesses us with fresh supplies
   Of joy out of salvation's wells.

Above what we can ask or hope
   The God of grace delights to give,
To fill the empty vessels up,
   To make us grace for grace receive.

THE CHRISTIAN EXPERIENCE

IN HIS FORGIVENESS

O GOD, forgivenesses are Thine
Far above all our hearts conceive;
The glorious property divine
Is still to pity and forgive;
With Thee is full redemption found,
And grace doth more than sin abound.

THOU art Thyself the seal;
   I more than pardon feel,
Peace, unutterable peace,
   Joy that ages ne'er can move,
Faith's assurance, hope's increase,
   All the confidence of love.

IN HIS POWER TO DESTROY SIN AND CREATE VIRTUE

MAY I, may all who humbly wait,
   Thy glorious joy receive,
Joy above all conception great,
   Worthy of God to give.

With confidence I now look up,
   Thy promised aid implore.
Sweetly revive my blasted hope,
   And I can doubt no more.

The dreadful, dire, oppressive hour
   Of tyrant sin is past;
My soul defies its rage and power,
   My soul on Thee is cast.

The power of hell, the strength of sin,
   Thou Jesu wilt subdue;
Thy healing blood shall wash me clean
   And make my spirit new.

CONFIDENCE IN GOD

No longer am I now afraid;
 Thy promise must take place.
Perfect Thy strength in weakness made,
 Sufficient is Thy grace.

Confident now of faith's increase,
 I all its fruits shall prove:
Substantial joy, and settled peace,
 And everlasting love.

Lord, I believe and rest secure
 In confidence divine;
Thy promise stands for ever sure,
 And all Thou art is mine.

As MY day my strength hath been
 And shall for ever be;
Grace, an overmatch for sin,
 Will still deliver me.
Every day the truth I prove
Of Jesus my almighty Friend,
 Kept by Him, whose constant love
 Shall keep me to the end.

I shall every day receive
 Sufficient strength of grace,
Always in His Spirit to live
 And walk in all His ways:
While I thus in faith go on,
I shall not sin's desires fulfil,
 Strong through Him to tread them down
 And do His utmost will.

On His strength do I lay hold,
 And walk in Christ my way,
Through Him confident, and bold
 His perfect law to obey;
I shall do His utmost will,
As sure as God is wholly true,
 Compass the impossible
 Which Jesus bids me do.

THE CHRISTIAN EXPERIENCE

QUICKENED with our immortal Head,
  Who daily, Lord, ascend with Thee,
Redeemed from sin and free indeed,
  We taste our glorious liberty;
Saved from the fear of hell and death,
  With joy we seek the things above,
And with Thy saints the Spirit breathe
  Of power, sobriety, and love.

Power o'er the world, the fiend and sin
  We in Thy gracious Spirit feel,
Full power the victory to win
  And answer all Thy righteous will.
Pure love to God Thy members find,
  Pure love to every soul of man;
And in Thy sober spotless mind,
  Saviour, our heaven on earth we gain.

CHRIST for ever lives to pray
  For all that trust in Him;
I my soul on Jesus stay,
  Almighty to redeem.
He shall purify my heart,
Who in His blood forgiveness have,
All His hallowing power exert,
  And to the utmost save.

THE FIRST faint spark of good desire
Which feebly would to heaven aspire
  Its kindler, God, will not despise;
The spark into a flame shall spread,
And blessed by Him the smallest seed
  Of faith into a tree shall rise.

CONFIDENCE IN GOD

This dawn of grace, this glimmering ray,
Shall shine unto the perfect day,
  For faithful Thou my Saviour art;
And I who tremble at Thy word
Shall find my paradise restored,
  Shall love my God with all my heart.

IN HIS POWER TO KEEP TO THE END

THE LIVING principle of grace,
The faith producing holiness,
  Now in our hearts doth dwell;
And still it shall in us abide,
Till saved, and wholly sanctified,
  We all Thy fulness feel.

Jesus, we steadfastly believe
The grace Thou dost this moment give
  Thou wilt the next bestow;
Wilt keep us every moment here,
And show Thyself the Finisher,
  And never let us go.

I KNOW in whom I have believed,
  Who, when this precious faith He gave,
My soul into His hands received,
  And bade me trust His power to save.

His Spirit doth my heart assure
  That what I still to Him commend
His constant love shall keep secure,
  Till faith filled up in vision end.

THE CHRISTIAN EXPERIENCE

IN HIS VICTORY

Away with our fears!
The Almighty appears,
Our Captain and Head.
We are all to infallible victory led.

In His Spirit alone
We are bold to go on,
His victory share,
And by patience o'ercome the afflictions we bear.

We with Jesus endure,
Till for glory mature
Our souls we resign,
And ascend to partake of the triumph divine.

Jesu, my soul takes hold on Thee,
   I arm me with Thy Spirit's might;
Humbly assured of victory,
   I underneath Thy banner fight.

IN HIS PERFECTING OF THE CHURCH

Our Jesus is gone up on high,
   And gifts He hath received for men;
He sends His Spirit to purify
   Our souls from every sinful stain.

Teachers He gives our souls to feed,
   The word of truth and grace to impart,
Dispensers of the living bread
   And pastors after His own heart.

He makes them apt to teach, and guide
   The flock with wisdom from above,
Till all are wholly sanctified
   Through faith, and perfected in love.

CONFIDENCE IN GOD

The glorious ministry divine
    For this he did on earth ordain,
Nor can He miss of His design
    Or send His messengers in vain.

They, under Him, His Church shall build,
    And lead His feeblest people on,
Till all our souls with God are filled,
    For ever sanctified in one.

Believing on our common Lord,
    We shall His image here regain,
Experience His utmost word,
    Be brought unto a perfect man.

By that which every joint supplies
    The whole shall still increase and move,
Till all complete the body rise,
    Now perfectly built up in love.

IN THE COMING OF HIS KINGDOM

BEHOLD the mighty Prince of peace.
    His peace and power to all extend;
His power shall evermore increase
    And never shall His mercies end.
His mercies flow to all mankind;
    His arms of love would all embrace;
And every soul of man may find
    The power of His all-pardoning grace.

He will the steadfast mind impart,
    The power that never shall remove,
Make firm in every sinless heart
    His throne of everlasting love,
Bring in the kingdom of His peace,
    Fill all our souls with joy unknown,
And 'stablish us in righteousness,
    And perfect all His saints in one.

THE CHRISTIAN EXPERIENCE

IN HIS REWARD

CONQUEROR of sin and hell and death,
    As Thou the dreadful fight hast won,
And wearest now the immortal wreath,
    And sittest on Thy Father's throne,

So shalt Thou grant to all that fight
    And conquer in Thy mighty name,
To claim the kingdom as their right,
    Their sufferings and their crown the same.

Who bore Thy cross shall wear Thy crown,
    Shall triumph in Thy victory,
And in Thy glorious throne sit down
    And reign in endless bliss with Thee.

The Life of the Church

THE SERVICES OF THE CHURCH

AT PUBLIC WORSHIP

HEAD of the Church, appear, appear,
Assembled with Thy members here,
Who in Thy name and Spirit meet
And tremble at Thy wounded feet.

O'ercome, o'erwhelmed with mercy's power,
We meekly wonder and adore,
With silent awe Thy goodness prove,
Or triumph in Thy dying love.

Whene'er Thou dost Thy love reveal,
Unutterable bliss we feel,
We feel the virtue of Thy name
In holy fear and humble shame.

Constrained by pure delight we own
The everlasting life begun,
Glory anticipate in grace
And heaven in Thy smiling face.

    SAVIOUR and Friend of men,
      Be still benignly near,
    And us to life ordain
      Who now Thy gospel hear;
    Incline us to depart from sin,
    And thus Thy grace and glory win.

    Our broken hearts prepare
      By deepest poverty,
    And then, by entering there,
      Dispose to yield to Thee;
    Make us to righteousness aspire,
    And draw to Thee our whole desire.

THE LIFE OF THE CHURCH

Ordained, prepared, disposed,
  By Thy preventing grace,
May we, our hearts unclosed,
  Thy gospel truth embrace;
Our proffered Lord may we receive,
And with triumphant joy believe.

SING, ye happy souls, that press
  Toward the height of holiness.
Praise Him whom in part ye know;
Freely to His goodness flow;
  All His promises receive,
  All the grace He hath to give.

Jointly, Lord, we come to Thee,
All in one request agree:
Feed us with the living Bread,
With Thyself our spirits feed;
Give the unction from above,
Oil of joy, and wine of love.

AFTER WORSHIP

ACTIONS He more than words requires,
  Actions with right intention done,
Good works the fruit of good desires,
  Obedience to His will alone,
Pure hope which seeks the things above,
Practical faith, and real love.

Let us, on whom His blessings flow,
  Our faith's integrity approve
By practising the truths we know
  With humble zeal and fervent love,
And live to show our Master's praise,
And die to glorify His grace.

THE SERVICES OF THE CHURCH

AT A FELLOWSHIP MEETING

GLORY be to God above,
   God, from whom all blessings flow.
Make we mention of His love,
   Publish we His praise below;
Called together by His grace,
   We are met in Jesu's name,
See with joy each other's face,
   Followers of the conquering Lamb.

Build we each the other up;
   Pray we for our faith's increase,
Lasting comfort, steadfast hope,
   Solid joy, and settled peace.
More and more let love abound;
   Never, never may we rest,
Till we are in Jesus found,
   Of our paradise possessed.

He will not His gifts delay
   If we patiently endure,
Will not empty send away
   Sinners hungry, mournful, poor.
Drink and eat, my well-beloved;
   Lean, He cries, upon my breast,
Till ye all, from earth removed,
   Share with Me the marriage-feast.

WHEN PARTED FROM THE FELLOWSHIP

CHRIST, our Head and common Lord,
   See the souls that wait on Thee;
Hear us all with one accord
   Sweetly in Thy praise agree;
Parted though in flesh we are,
   Joined to Thee, our Corner-stone,
We are intimately near,
   Present, and in spirit one.

THE LIFE OF THE CHURCH

Let us now to Thee aspire,
    Who Thy life begin to know;
Let the circulating fire
    Now in every bosom glow.
Faithfully on Thee we call:
    Perfect all our souls in one;
With us, by us, in us all
    Joyfully Thy will be done.

AT THE BAPTISM OF INFANTS

JESUS, in earth and heaven the same,
    Accept a parent's vow;
To Thee, baptized into Thy name,
    I bring my children now.
Thy love permits, invites, commands
    My offspring to be blessed;
Lay on them, Lord, Thy gracious hands,
    And hide them in Thy breast.

To all the hallowing Spirit give
    Even from their infancy,
And pure into Thy Church receive
    Whom I devote to Thee.
Committed to Thy faithful care,
    Protected by Thy blood,
Preserve by Thine unceasing prayer
    And bring them all to God.

LORD of all, with pure intent,
    From his tenderest infancy,
In Thy temple I present
    Whom I first received from Thee.
Through Thy well-beloved Son,
Mine acknowledge for Thine own.

THE SERVICES OF THE CHURCH

Sealed with the baptismal seal,
Purchased with the atoning blood,
Jesus in my infant dwell;
Make his heart the house of God.
Fill Thy consecrated shrine,
Father, Son, and Spirit Divine.

AT THE BAPTISM OF AN ADULT

FATHER, Son and Holy Ghost,
　In solemn power come down,
Present with Thy heavenly host
　Thine ordinance to crown.

Let the promised inward grace
　Accompany the sign,
On this new-born soul impress
　The glorious name divine.

Father, all Thy love reveal,
　Jesus, all Thy mind impart,
Holy Ghost, renew, and dwell
　For ever in his heart.

AT HOLY COMMUNION

SAVIOUR, Thy flesh is meat indeed.
　Thy nature, to Thy Church made known,
Doth every saint with manna feed
　Till every saint with Thee is one,
Till blended with its heavenly food
　The soul Thy gracious fulness feels,
And all transformed we dwell in God,
　And God in us for ever dwells.

THE LIFE OF THE CHURCH

For sure as Thee through faith we eat,
  Thy Spirit's substance we receive,
And one with our mysterious meat
  Through all eternity shall live.
Give us on Thee, the living Bread,
  To live till here our journeys end;
Thou Bread of heaven, Thy pilgrims lead
  To realms from which Thou didst descend.

Come, Holy Ghost, set to Thy seal,
  Thine inward witness give;
To all our waiting souls reveal
  The death by which we live.

Spectators of the pangs divine
  Oh make us now to be,
Discerning in the sacred sign
  Christ's Passion on the tree.

Repeat the Saviour's dying cry
  In every heart so loud
That every heart may now reply,
  This was the Son of God.

Come, all who truly bear
  The name of Christ your Lord,
His last mysterious Supper share
  And keep His kindest word.
Hereby your faith approve
  In Jesus crucified;
In memory of My dying love
  Do this, He said, and died.

The badge and token this,
  The sure confirming seal
That He is ours and we are His,
  The servants of His will,

THE SERVICES OF THE CHURCH

His dear beloved ones,
The purchase of His blood,
His blood which once for all atones
And brings us now to God.

Then let us still profess
Our Master's honoured name,
Stand forth His faithful witnesses,
True followers of the Lamb.
In proof that such we are,
His saying we receive,
And thus to all mankind declare
We do in Christ believe.

Part of His Church below,
We thus our right maintain;
Our living membership we show
And in the fold remain.
We with His sheep are told,
With all His people fed,
And fellowship with all we hold
Who hold it with our Head.

JESU, Thy weakest servant bless;
Give what these hallowed signs express,
  And what Thou giv'st secure.
Pardon into my soul convey,
Strength in Thy pardoning love to stay,
  And to the end endure.

Raise, and enable me to stand;
Save out of the destroyer's hand
  This helpless soul of mine.
Vouchsafe me then Thy strengthening grace,
And with the arms of love embrace,
  And keep me ever Thine.

THE LIFE OF THE CHURCH

O GOD of truth and love,
Let us Thy mercy prove.
Bless Thine Ordinance divine,
Let it now effectual be;
Answer all its great design,
All its gracious ends, in me.

O may the sacred Word
Set forth our dying Lord,
Point us to Thy sufferings past,
Present grace and strength impart,
Give our ravished souls a taste,
Pledge of glory in our heart.

Come in Thy Spirit down;
Thine Institution crown.
Lamb of God, as slain appear,
Life of all believers Thou;
Let us now perceive Thee near;
Come, Thou Hope of glory, now.

How LONG, Thou faithful God, shall I
Here in Thy ways forgotten lie?
When shall the means of healing be
The channels of Thy grace to me?

Angel and Son of God, come down,
Thy Sacramental Banquet crown;
Thy power into the means infuse,
And give them now their sacred use.

Break to me now the hallowed Bread,
And bid me on Thy Body feed;
Give me the Wine, Almighty God,
And let me drink Thy precious Blood.

THE SERVICES OF THE CHURCH

COME, let us join with one accord,
Who share the Supper of the Lord,
   Our Lord and Master's praise to sing.
Nourished on earth with Living Bread,
We now are at His Table fed,
   But wait for heaven to see our King;
To see the great Invisible
Without a Sacramental veil,
   With all His robes of glory on;
In rapturous joy and love and praise,
Him to behold with open face,
   High on His everlasting throne.

The Wine which doth His Passion shew,
We then with Him shall drink it new
   In yonder dazzling courts above;
Admitted to the heavenly Feast,
We shall His choicest blessings taste
   And banquet on His richest love.
By faith and hope already there,
Ev'n now the marriage Feast we share,
   Ev'n now we by the Lamb are fed;
Our Lord's celestial joy we prove,
Led by the spirit of His love,
   To springs of living comfort led.

HAPPY the souls that followed Thee
Lamenting Thy accursed rood,
Happy who underneath the tree
Unmovable in sorrow stood.

Oh what a time for offering up
Their souls upon Thy Sacrifice!
Who would not with Thy burden stoop,
And bow the head when Jesus dies?

THE LIFE OF THE CHURCH

Yet in this ordinance divine
We still the sacred load may bear;
And now we in Thy offering join,
Thy sacramental passion share.

Thou art with all Thy members here;
In this tremendous mystery
We jointly before God appear
To offer up ourselves with Thee.

AND SHALL I let Him go?
If now I do not *feel*
The streams of Living Water flow,
Shall I forsake the Well?

Because He hides His face,
Shall I no longer stay,
But leave the channels of His grace
And cast the means away?

Jesus hath spoke the Word;
His will my reason is:
Do this in memory of thy Lord,
Jesus hath said, Do this.

He bids me eat the Bread;
He bids me drink the Wine.
No other motive, Lord, I need,
No other Word than Thine.

I cheerfully comply
With what my Lord doth say.
Let others ask a reason why;
My glory is to obey.

Because He saith, Do this,
This I will always do;
Till Jesus come in glorious bliss
I thus His death will show.

THE SERVICES OF THE CHURCH

Sons of God, triumphant rise;
Shout the accomplish'd sacrifice.
Shout your sins in Christ forgiven,
Sons of God, and heirs of heaven.

Ye that round our altars throng,
Listening angels, join the song;
Sing with us, ye heavenly powers,
Pardon, grace, and glory ours.

Love's mysterious work is done;
Greet we now the accepted Son,
Healed and quicken'd by His blood,
Joined to Christ, and one with God.

AT AN ORDINATION

Great triune God, Thy servants own;
And while they make Thy nature known,
    Let them Thy promised presence find—
Sent to baptize into Thy name,
Sent a lost world for Thine to claim,
    Sent to disciple all mankind.

With signs their high commission seal;
In every ordinance reveal
    Thyself, and shed Thy love abroad.
Their apostolic labours crown;
Come Father, Son, and Spirit down,
    And fill our universe with God.

AT CONFERENCE

Arise, all-seeing God, arise,
    Thy sifting power exert,
Look through us with Thy flaming eyes,
    And search out every heart.

THE LIFE OF THE CHURCH

If still we in Thy grace abide,
   Our call confirm and clear,
And into Thy whole counsel guide
   Thy poorest messenger.

Unite our hearts to all that bear
   The burden of the Lord,
And let our spotless lives declare
   The virtue of Thy word.

One soul into us all inspire,
   And let it strongly move
In fervent flames of calm desire
   To glorify Thy love.

Oh may we in Thy love agree,
   To make its sweetness known;
Thy love the bond of union be,
   And perfect us in one.

O LORD, our strength and righteousness,
   Our base and head and corner-stone,
Our peace with God, our mutual peace,
   Unite, and keep Thy servants one,
That while we speak in Jesu's name,
We all may speak and think the same.

That Spirit of love to each impart,
   That fervent mind, which was in Thee;
So shall we all our strength exert,
   In heart and word and deed agree
To advance the kingdom of Thy grace,
And spread Thine everlasting praise.

Now, Lord, to Thine almighty hand
   The keeping of our hearts we give,
Firm in one mind and spirit stand,
   To Thee and to each other cleave,
Fixed on the Rock which cannot move,
And meekly safe in humble love.

THE SERVICES OF THE CHURCH

O most compassionate High-priest,
  Thy tempted messengers defend;
Honoured, exposed, above the rest,
  To us Thy timely succour send;
With each in his temptation stay,
Nor cast one helpless soul away.

Save us from pride and worldly love,
  From envy mean and base desire;
Our lust of praise and power remove;
  Walk with Thy servants in the fire;
Appear our Leader on the flood,
Support us with the arm of God.

Entering into our closet, Lord,
  Thee let us daily seek and find,
Studious to preach and live Thy word,
  To copy out Thy perfect mind,
To be as Thou our Master art,
Lowly and meek and pure in heart.

Our privilege to deal
Supersubstantial bread,
And with Thy meat invisible
Poor hungry souls to feed,
By ministering Thy word
Thy flock to multiply,
And with the Spirit of our Lord
The growing Church supply.

Our call is to dispense
Thy blessings from above,
The peace of cancelled guilt, the sense
Of holy joy and love.
Let the full proof appear
In multitudes forgiven,
Help us to save the souls that hear,
Help us to people heaven.

THE LIFE OF THE CHURCH

AT A FUNERAL

BLESSING, honour, thanks, and praise,
   Pay we, gracious God, to Thee;
Thou in Thine abundant grace
   Givest us the victory.
True and faithful to Thy word,
   Thou hast glorified Thy Son;
Jesus Christ, our dying Lord,
   He for us the fight hath won.

Yes, the Christian's course is run,
   Ended is the glorious strife,
Fought the fight, the work is done,
   Death is swallowed up in life;
Borne by angels on their wings,
   Far from earth the spirit flies,
Finds his God, and sits and sings
   Triumphing in paradise.

Let the world bewail their dead,
   Fondly of their loss complain;
Brother, friend, by Jesus freed,
   Death to thee, to us, is gain.
Thou art enter'd into joy;
   Let the unbelievers mourn;
We in songs our lives employ,
   Till we all to God return.

COME let us who in Christ believe
   With saints and angels join,
Glory and praise and blessing give
   And thanks to Love divine.

Our friend in sure and certain hope
   Hath laid his body down;
He knew that Christ would raise him up
   And give the victor's crown.

THE SERVICES OF THE CHURCH

To all who His appearing love
  He opens paradise;
We too shall join the hosts above,
  We too shall grasp the prize.

Then let us wait to see the day,
  To hear the joyful word,
To answer: Lo, we come away;
  We die to meet our Lord.

WHEN from flesh the spirit freed
  Hastens homeward to return,
Mortals cry, 'A man is dead'
  Angels sing, 'A child is born.'

Born into the world above,
  They our happy brother greet,
Bear him to the throne of love,
  Place him at the Saviour's feet.

Jesus smiles, and says, 'Well done,
  Good and faithful servant thou.
Enter and receive Thy crown;
  Reign with Me triumphant now.'

GLORY be to God on high,
God in whom we live and die,
God who guides us by His love,
Takes us to His throne above.
Angels that surround His throne,
Sing the wonders He hath done,
Shout while we on earth reply:
Glory be to God on high.

God of everlasting grace,
Worthy Thou of endless praise;
Thou hast all Thy blessings shed
On the living and the dead.

THE LIFE OF THE CHURCH

Thou wast here their sure defence;
Thou hast borne their spirits hence;
Worthy Thou of endless praise,
God of everlasting grace.

Thanks be all ascribed to Thee,
Blessing, power, and majesty,
Thee, by whose almighty name
They their latest foe o'ercame.
Thou the victory hast won,
Saved them by Thy grace alone,
Caught them up Thy face to see;
Thanks be all ascribed to Thee.

Happy in Thy glorious love,
We too shall from earth remove;
Glad partakers of our hope,
We shall soon be taken up,
Meet again our heavenly friends,
Blest with bliss that never ends,
Joined to all Thy hosts above,
Happy in Thy glorious love.

THOU out of great distress
　　To thy reward art passed,
Triumphant happiness,
　　And joys that always last.
Thanks be to God, who set thee free,
And gave the final victory.

Thy victory we share;
　　Thy glorious joy we feel.
Parted in flesh we are,
　　But joined in spirit still;
And still we on our brethren call
To praise the common Lord of all.

THE SERVICES OF THE CHURCH

Thus let us still maintain
Our fellowship divine,
And till we meet again
In Jesu's praises join;
Thus, till we all your raptures know,
Sing you above, and we below.

THE CHURCH'S YEAR

ADVENT

SING with glad anticipation;
Mortals and immortals sing.
Jesus comes with full salvation;
Jesus doth His glory bring.
Hallelujah!
God omnipotent is King!

See, ye heirs of sure salvation,
Jesu's most majestic grace,
At His final revelation,
While in triumph He displays
All His glories,
All the Godhead in His face.

To His royal proclamation
Manifested here, attend;
In His state of exaltation
While He doth with clouds descend,
Brings the kingdom,
Gives the joy that ne'er shall end.

Power is all to Jesus given;
All His foes must fall before
The great King of earth and heaven,
When He takes His royal power.
Lord, assume it;
Jesus, reign for evermore.

THE LIFE OF THE CHURCH

LET us triumphantly ride on
  And more than conquerors prove,
With meekness bear the opposers down
  And bind with cords of love.

Then, only then, our eyes shall see
  Thy promised kingdom come;
And every heart, by grace set free,
  Shall make the Saviour room.

Thee every tongue shall then confess,
  And every knee shall bow.
Come quickly, Lord, we wait Thy grace;
  We long to meet Thee now.

JESU, descend again
  With all Thy heavenly train;
Our eternal life appear
  With Thy robes of glory on;
Manifest Thy kingdom here;
  Take us up into Thy throne.

Now let Thy face be seen,
  Without a veil between.
Come and change our faith to sight;
  Swallow up mortality;
Plunge us in a sea of light;
  Christ, be all in all to me.

LORD, our life of faith and prayer
  Will languish soon and die,
If Thou dost not still repair
  And with fresh grace supply.
That we still in Thee may live,
  Be Thou Thyself our daily Bread;
Every hour Thy Spirit give
  And every moment feed.

THE CHURCH'S YEAR

Keep us to that solemn hour
When Thou the Judge shalt come;
Then through Thine almighty power
We triumph o'er the tomb.
In the twinkling of an eye,
Caught up, on eagles' wings we soar,
Swiftly to Thy presence fly,
And meet to part no more.

Then we eat before Thy throne
The immortalizing Food,
Glorious joy till then unknown,
In the full sight of God,
Drink the new celestial wine,
Banquet with all the saints above,
Satisfied with Truth divine
And pure eternal Love.

CHRISTMAS

THE LAMB from the throne
Of His Father came down;
He was flesh of our flesh, He was bone of our bone.

The omnipotent Lord
By all heaven adored,
The invisible Godhead, appeared in the Word.

He came from on high,
Who fashioned the sky,
And meekly vouchsafed in a manger to lie.

Who gave all things to be,
What a wonder to see
Him born of His creature, and nursed on her knee!

So heavenly mild
His innocence smiled,
No wonder the mother should worship the Child.

THE LIFE OF THE CHURCH

The angels she knew
Had worshipped Him too,
And still they confess adoration His due.

The shepherds behold
Him promised of old,
By angels attended, by prophets foretold.

The wise men adore
And bring Him their store;
The rich are permitted to follow the poor.

We too on His face,
With eager amaze
And pleasure ecstatic, now worshipping gaze.

Our newly born King,
Transported, we sing,
And heaven and earth with the triumph doth ring.

GOD IN MORTAL flesh revealed,
    Explain the mystery.
Show it still on man fulfilled;
    Be manifest in me.
Thou who didst on earth appear,
By faith conceived, Thyself impart;
    Pitch Thy tabernacle here
    In my believing heart.

Thou, who didst so greatly stoop
    To a poor virgin's womb,
Here Thy mean abode take up;
    To me, my Saviour, come.
Come, and Satan's works destroy,
And let me all Thy Godhead prove,
    Filled with peace and heavenly joy
    And pure eternal love.

THE CHURCH'S YEAR

Then my soul with strange delight
    Shall comprehend and feel
All the length, and breadth, and height
    Of love unspeakable;
Then I shall the secret know
Which angels would search out in vain:
    God was man, and served below,
        That man with God might reign.

He is wrapped in swaddling bands
    Who with darkness swathes the sea,
Who the universe commands,
    Comprehends immensity.

Triumph we the sons of grace
    That our God is born so poor,
Doth His majesty abase
    Our salvation to secure.

Glorying in our infant King,
    Him we in the manger own,
Him whom brightest seraphs sing,
    High on His eternal throne.

Celebrate Immanuel's name,
    The Prince of life and peace;
God with us our lips proclaim,
    Our faithful hearts confess.
God is in our flesh revealed;
Heaven and earth in Jesus join;
    Mortal with immortal filled,
        And human with divine.

Fulness of the Deity
    In Jesu's body dwells,
Dwells in all His saints and me,
    When God His Son reveals.

THE LIFE OF THE CHURCH

Father, manifest Thy Son,
And, conscious of the incarnate Word,
In our inmost souls make known
The presence of the Lord.

Let the Spirit of our Head
 Through every member flow;
By our Lord inhabited,
 We then Immanuel know;
Then He doth His name express
And God in us we truly prove,
 Filled with all the life of grace
 And all the power of love.

REJOICE in Jesu's birth.
 To us a Son is given;
To us a Child is born on earth
 Who made both earth and heaven.

The Almighty God is He,
 Author of heavenly bliss,
The Father of eternity,
 The glorious Prince of Peace.

Wider and wider still
 He doth His sway extend,
With peace divine His people fill
 And joys that never end.

His government shall grow,
 From strength to strength proceed,
His righteousness the Church o'erflow
 And all the earth o'erspread.

His presence shall increase
 The happiness above,
The full, progressive happiness
 Of everlasting love.

THE CHURCH'S YEAR

THE SOLEMN hour is come
For God made visible,
Fruit of a virgin's womb,
A man with men to dwell,
The Saviour of the world to appear
And found His heavenly kingdom here.

Let all mankind abase
  Their souls before the Lord;
And humbly prostrate, praise
  The great incarnate Word;
And welcome Jesus from above
With joy and gratitude and love.

HAPPY who the angel's word
  Hesitate not to believe,
Who their mean almighty Lord,
  God in swaddling-clothes receive.
O Thou heavenly Man divine,
  Grant me their simplicity,
Then before Thy humble shrine
  All my soul shall worship Thee.

EPIPHANY

HAIL, holy, heaven-descended Child,
Who God and man hast reconciled,
  Whom angels bow before!
Whate'er I have of good to give,
To Thee, from whom I first receive,
  I thankfully restore.

To Thee my heart I open wide;
The myrrh of passions mortified,
  The gold of charity,
The incense sweet of humble prayer,
I now, Thy prostrate worshipper,
  With joy present to Thee.

THE LIFE OF THE CHURCH

PALM SUNDAY

SION, rejoice thy King to see;
  Meekness and love compose His train.
By patience and humility,
  He comes o'er willing hearts to reign.
Ye need not fear the sinner's Friend
Who comes your sins and fears to end.

Sinners by gentleness He wins
  And sweetly bends them to His sway.
Receive your mild pacific Prince;
  Enjoy the happiness to obey;
Delight His easy yoke to prove,
And bless His law of life and love.

OUR KING we now go forth to meet,
And Jesus with Hosannahs greet.
He comes, He comes on earth to reign;
He brings us back our power again.

In us who Christ our God adore
He doth His kingdom here restore,
And in our faithful hearts we prove
The reigning power of Jesu's love.

The Author of our joy we bless,
The King of peace and righteousness,
Triumphant in the earnest given,
For present love is present heaven.

We soon shall meet Him in the sky
And ceaseless Hallelujah cry,
Palms in our hands as conquerors bear
And glory on our foreheads wear.

THE CHURCH'S YEAR

GENTLE and meek He comes to those
   In compassing His death employed,
His furious, unrelenting foes
   Who thirsted for their Saviour's blood;
Gives Himself up to satisfy
Their rage and for His murderers die.

Oh how unlike the kingdoms here
   Is that Thou openest in Thine own!
Meekness and peace and lowly fear
   And righteousness support Thy throne,
Patience in death, resembling Thine,
And love invincibly divine.

GOOD FRIDAY

'TIS FINISHED! The Messiah dies,
   Cut off for sins, but not His own.
Accomplished is the sacrifice;
   The great redeeming work is done.

The veil is rent in Christ alone;
   The living way to heaven is seen;
The middle wall is broken down,
   And all mankind may enter in.

The reign of sin and death is o'er,
   And all may live from sin set free;
Satan hath lost his mortal power;
   'Tis swallowed up in victory.

HAPPY might I stationed be
Near the ignominious tree!
Lamb of God my prayer admit,
Place me at Thy wounded feet.

THE LIFE OF THE CHURCH

Here I would through life abide,
Watching with the Crucified,
Fixed in silent wonder gaze
On Thy marred yet heavenly face.

Give me thus Thy death to see,
Till my soul is all like Thee,
Meet to live the life above,
Swallowed up in praise and love.

JESUS by pangs of death oppressed
With outstretched hands the pillars seized;
Compassed with foes He bowed His head,
For mercy, not for vengeance, prayed,
And groaned His last expiring groan,
And pulled the infernal kingdom down.

LORD, that every moment I
May on Thy dear cross rely,
Still the mystery reveal
Of Thy love unspeakable.

What Thou gav'st me once to know
Oh continue to bestow;
Give me, every moment give,
By Thy precious death to live.

This my sole employment be,
Stationed here on Calvary:
Let me on Thy passion gaze,
See Thee dying in my place.

While I thus my Pattern view,
I shall bleed and suffer too,
With the Man of sorrow joined
One become in heart and mind,

THE CHURCH'S YEAR

More and more like Jesus grow,
Till the Finisher I know,
Gain the final victor's wreath,
Perfect love in perfect death.

O JESUS, let Thy dying cry
　　Pierce to the bottom of my heart,
Its evils cure, its wants supply,
　　And bid its unbelief depart,
Slay the dire root and seed of sin,
　　Prepare for Thee the holiest place;
Then, then, essential Love, come in,
　　And fill Thy house with endless praise.

OH LET Thy death's mysterious power
　　With all its sacred weight descend
To consecrate my final hour,
　　To bless me with Thy peaceful end;
And breathed into the hands divine,
My spirit be received with Thine.

GREATER love is not in man,
　　But greater is in God;
Life for sinners to regain
　　Jehovah sheds His blood,
Gives Himself a sacrifice,
　　His own most precious blood expends,
Freely for His foes He dies,
　　And turns them into friends.

THE HOLY Jesus rests in hope,
　　And calm in death on God relies;
His parting spirit He gives up
　　Into His Father's hands, and dies.

THE LIFE OF THE CHURCH

Meek, patient Lamb, for us He gives
  The life which none could take away,
And lays it down, and God receives
  His soul into eternal day.

Oh may I thus my warfare end,
  Meekly the things of earth resign,
And to God's hands my soul commend.
  O Jesus, let Thy death be mine.

EASTER DAY

THE LORD of life is risen indeed,
To death delivered in your stead;
His rise proclaims your sins forgiven
And shows the living way to heaven.

Haste then, ye souls that first believe,
Who dare the gospel word receive,
Your faith with joyful hearts confess;
Be bold, be Jesu's witnesses.

Go tell the followers of your Lord
Their Jesus is to life restored;
He lives, that they His life may find;
He lives to quicken all mankind.

AMONG the dead in vain
  Ye seek your heavenly Lord;
He lives, He lives again
  According to His word!
Receive the power His life imparts,
And find Him risen in your hearts.

THE CHURCH'S YEAR

FATHER, God, we glorify
   Thy love to Adam's seed,
Love that gave Thy Son to die
   And raised Him from the dead;
Him for our offences slain,
   That we all might pardon find,
Thou hast brought to life again,
   The Saviour of mankind.

By Thy own right hand of power
   Thou hast exalted Him,
Sent the mighty Conqueror
   Thy people to redeem;
King of saints and Prince of peace,
   Him Thou hast to sinners given,
Sinners from their sins to bless
   And lift them up to heaven.

Father, God, to us impart
   The gift unspeakable;
Now in every waiting heart
   Thy glorious Son reveal.
Quickened with our living Lord,
   Let us in Thy Spirit rise,
Rise to all Thy life restored,
   And thank Thee in the skies.

   COME, ye that seek the Lord,
     Him that was crucified,
  Come listen to the gospel word
     And feel it now applied.
   To every soul of man
     The joyful news we show:
  Jesus, for every sinner slain,
     Is risen again for you.

   Salvation we proclaim
     Which every soul may find,
  Pardon and peace in Jesu's name,
     And life for all mankind.

THE LIFE OF THE CHURCH

He lives, who spilt His blood;
Believe our record true.
The Arm, the Power, the Son of God
Shall be revealed in you.

CHRIST, our living Head, draw near;
　At our call, Quicken all
　　Thy true members here.

Filled with faith's eternal Spirit,
　Grant that we, Dead with Thee,
　　May Thy life inherit.

All Thy resurrection's power,
　All Thy love, From above,
　　On Thy servants shower.

Partners of Thy death and passion,
　Oh that we All may see
　　All Thy great salvation.

Children of the resurrection,
　Lead us on To the crown
　　Of our full perfection.

There, where Thou art gone before us,
　Christ, our Hope, Take us up;
　　To Thy heaven restore us.

ASCENSION DAY

COME let us rise with Christ our Head
　And seek the things above,
By the almighty Spirit led
　And filled with faith and love;
Our hearts detached from all below
　Should after Him ascend,
And only wish the joy to know
　Of our triumphant Friend.

THE CHURCH'S YEAR

Enthroned at God's right hand He sits,
  Maintainer of our cause,
Till every vanquished foe submits
  To His victorious cross;
Worthy to be exalted thus
  The Lamb for sinners slain,
The Lord our King, who reigns for us,
  And shall for ever reign.

To Him our willing hearts we give
  Who gives us power and peace,
And dead to sin, His members live
  The life of righteousness;
The hidden life of Christ is ours
  With Christ concealed above,
And tasting the celestial powers
  We banquet on His love.

LIFT up your heads, ye gates,
  To admit your King again.
Returned from earth, He waits
  With half His angel train.
Wide open throw the heavenly scene;
Receive the King of glory in.

Instinct with living powers
  The huge portcullis raise;
Ye everlasting doors,
  Disclose the holiest place.
Wide open throw the heavenly scene;
Receive the King of glory in.

He comes, He comes from far,
  The strong and mighty Lord,
Mighty and strong in war,
  To claim His just reward.
Wide open throw the heavenly scene;
Receive the King of glory in.

THE LIFE OF THE CHURCH

The Lord of Hosts is He,
  The omnipotent I AM,
Glorious in majesty,
  Jehovah is His name.
Wide open throw the heavenly scene;
Receive the King of glory in.

Jehovah, Jesus, Lord
  Of earth and heaven receive,
Who comes that man, restored,
  With God again may live.
Wide open throw the heavenly scene;
Receive the King of glory in.

Forerunner of mankind,
  For us He reigns on high,
Till all His members joined
  Repeat the joyful cry:
Wide open throw the heavenly scene;
Receive the sons of glory in.

HE LIFTS the hands, stretched out so late
  And nailed to the accursed tree,
Which bore His sacred body's weight
  With all our sin and misery,
The hands from which our blessings flow,
  Which every creature's wants supply;
Fountains of grace to all below,
  They hold, and bear us to the sky.

Those hands, on which my hopes depend,
  My present, and eternal peace,
Lift up, and over me extend
  To guard and sanctify and bless;
Bless me from Thy celestial throne
  With more than heart can e'er conceive,
And seal, and take me for Thine own,
  Thy purchase, in Thy joy to live.

THE CHURCH'S YEAR

BEFORE WHITSUNDAY

JESUS, Thy weakest followers here,
  On whom Thou kindly hast bestowed
A principle of pious fear,
  A heart to seek our joy in God—
This smallest seed of love unfeigned
  We surely have received from Thee,
And tempted with our Lord remained,
  And hoped Thine utmost word to see.

While feebly in Thy paths we tread
  And most imperfectly obey,
Thy goodness and Thy truth we plead,
  And for the promised blessing pray;
Our day of Pentecost is nigh,
  Yet still it is not fully come
Till Thy good Spirit descend from high
  To make us His eternal home.

Father, who always hear'st our Friend
  And Advocate before Thy throne,
Vouchsafe that Paraclete to send,
  That Spirit of Thy spotless Son;
Ah give Him in our hearts to dwell,
  To fill with life, and love, and peace,
To constitute, and fix, and seal
  Our present and eternal bliss.

WHITSUNDAY

REJOICE, rejoice, ye fallen race,
  The day of Pentecost is come.
Expect the sure descending grace;
  Open your hearts to make Him room.

Our Jesus is gone up on high,
  For us the blessing to receive.
It now comes streaming from the sky;
  The Spirit comes, and sinners live.

THE LIFE OF THE CHURCH

Adore the grace unsearchable.
Long as eternal ages roll,
Our God delights in man to dwell,
The Soul of each believing soul.

JESU, we hang upon the word
   Our faithful souls have heard from Thee;
Be mindful of Thy promise, Lord,
   Thy promise made to all, and me:
Myself will to My orphans come,
And make you My eternal home.

Come, then, dear Lord, Thyself reveal,
   And let the promise now take place;
Be it according to Thy will,
   According to Thy word of grace;
Thy sorrowful disciples cheer,
And send us down the Comforter.

He visits now the troubled breast,
   And oft relieves our sad complaint,
But soon we lose the transient Guest,
   But soon we droop again and faint,
Our hearts are heavy as a stone,
Our joy is fled, our comfort gone.

Hasten Him, Lord, into our heart,
   Our sure inseparable Guide.
Oh may we meet and never part;
   Oh may He in our heart *abide*,
And keep His house of praise and prayer,
And rest and reign for ever there.

THE SPIRIT of our Head
Is on the members shed;
Ever streaming from above
He to us Thy name imparts,
Brings the unction from above,
Forms and dwells in Christian hearts.

THE CHURCH'S YEAR

Thy mystic body, we
Our all receive from Thee:
Life and truth, and grace for grace.
Thine anointed ones, we rise,
Temples of Thy holiness,
Filled with Him who fills the skies.

THE GOD of all grace,
To restore a lost race,
Hath raised up His Son
And hath sent Him again in the Comforter down.

God sent Him to bless
With unspeakable peace
The children of men,
That ye here may His favour and image regain.

Repent and believe
And the blessing receive,
The felicity pure,
The salvation of God which shall always endure.

STILL the Holy Ghost descends,
The indwelling Comforter,
All the griefs and troubles ends
Of those that Christ revere,
Works His miracles within,
Renews their hearts and tongues and eyes,
Makes an utter end of sin
And wholly sanctifies.

Always ready Thee we know
Thy mercy to reveal.
Saviour, now on us bestow
The gift unspeakable;
In the Comforter come down,
Who helps us for Himself to pray;
Take possession of Thine own,
And here for ever stay.

THE LIFE OF THE CHURCH

TRINITY SUNDAY

FATHER of all, we worship Thee;
 The God of glory is Thy name.
Jesus, the filial Deity,
 The Lord of glory we proclaim;
And the blest Spirit of holiness
The Spirit of glory we confess.

Come, Father, Son, and Holy Ghost,
 Whom one all-perfect God we own;
Restorer of Thine image lost,
 Thy various offices make known;
Display, our fallen souls to raise,
Thy whole economy of grace.

LET HEAVEN and earth agree
 The Father's praise to sing,
Who draws us to the Son, that He
 May us to glory bring.

Honour and endless love
 Let God the Son receive,
Who saves us here, and prays above,
 That we with Him may live.

Be everlasting praise
 To God the Spirit given,
Who now attests us sons of grace
 And seals us heirs of heaven.

Drawn and redeemed and sealed,
 We'll sing the One and Three,
With Father, Son, and Spirit filled
 To all eternity.

THE CHURCH'S YEAR

Father of our dear Lord,
   Thy mercy we record;
When Thou saw'st a world undone,
   Mercy freely Thee inclined,
Mercy gave Thine only Son,
   Death to taste for all mankind.

O Lamb, for sinners slain,
   For every soul of man,
Thou, for all men lifted up,
   Drawest all men unto Thee.
Glory be to Christ our Hope;
   All the world may hope in Thee.

Thee, Holy Ghost, we praise,
   Giver of general grace;
Preacher Thou to spirits bound
   Dost for hardened sinners grieve,
Those who, while He may be found,
   Will not come to God and live.

Blessing and praise to Thee,
   All-glorious Trinity.
Live by all Thy works adored,
   All below and all above,
Holy, holy, holy Lord,
   God of grace and God of love.

ALL SAINTS DAY

Thanks be to God who gave
   The victory and the prize.
Join, all who own His power to save,
   The triumph of the skies.
The Church of the first-born,
   To them by faith we come,
And conquerors of the world return
   To our celestial home.

THE LIFE OF THE CHURCH

We know in whom we trust,
We haste to His embrace,
Mixed with the spirits of the just,
The perfected in grace;
Their ripest joy to share,
Exulting we ascend,
And grasp our old companions there,
And our eternal Friend.

PRAYERS FOR THE CHURCH

FOR THE REVIVAL OF THE CHURCH

COME, O Thou Breath Divine,
From every quarter blow,
And whom Thou didst together join,
On them Thine influence show;
Thy wonder-working power
Be here again displayed,
And now to sudden life restore
The long-forgotten dead.

Inspired at God's command
By Thee, the Spirit of grace,
Let the whole house of Israel stand
And their Restorer praise;
Host of the living God,
Let them through earth declare
The heavenly Gift on all bestowed,
The indwelling Comforter.

FOR MEMBERS SUFFERING PERSECUTION

HEAD of Thy suffering Church below,
Give to Thy suffering people power;
Thy perfect strength in weakness show,
And arm them for the dreadful hour.

PRAYERS FOR THE CHURCH

To Thee let them in faith look up,
  And claim the succour from above,
And rise to all the strength of hope,
  To all the omnipotence of love.

Give them the indubitable sign
  That all their sufferings are for Thee;
Assure their hearts the cause is Thine,
  And Thou wilt get the victory.

Give them, before they bow the head,
  The sight to fervent Stephen given:
The everlasting doors displayed,
  The glories of a wide-spread heaven.

Show them Thyself at God's right hand;
  Thou on their faithful souls look down;
Thou by Thy dying champions stand,
  And reach them out the victor's crown.

Inspire them with Thy tender care
  For those who nailed Thee to the tree,
And give to their expiring prayer
  The men that drive their souls to Thee.

FOR MUTUAL LOVE

THE LOVE impartial and sincere,
The inimitable character
  On genuine saints impressed,
Oh that we in ourselves may find,
Endued with our Redeemer's mind,
  With His affection blessed.

Enlarged beyond the narrow space
Of those that their own sect embrace
  And none besides approve,
We would, to liberty restored,
Love all the lovers of our Lord
  And all who seek His love.

THE LIFE OF THE CHURCH

Jesus, the gospel-grace impart
To ours and every longing heart;
   Take us into Thy fold.
The truth of pure religion give,
That all who bear Thy name may live
   And love like those of old.

The mark on every face impress,
That like Thy first-born witnesses
   We hand in hand may move;
And ready each for each to die,
Constrain the world for each to cry,
   'See how these Christians love!'

To us the new command He gives.
   Oh may we all obedient prove
And take the legacy He leaves,
   His richest legacy of love.

Us each to other He commends
   And bids us in one Spirit join,
Unites, and makes us more than friends,
   All kinsmen, in a bond divine.

Give, Jesus, give the uniting grace,
   The bond of charity divine;
And let us all mankind embrace
   And love them with a love like Thine.

FOR UNITY

Obedient to our Lord's command,
Join every heart and every hand
   Of those who Jesus know,
To advance the kingdom of His grace,
To publish our Redeemer's praise,
   And spread His love below.

PRAYERS FOR THE CHURCH

Oh were we in Thy Spirit joined!
One heart, one judgement, and one mind
　To all Thy labourers give.
Unite us closer, Lord, to Thee,
That all may in Thy name agree
　And to Thy glory live;

That all may think and speak the same,
Jointly our common Lord proclaim,
　Our mission fully prove,
Determined Thee alone to know,
And to the world the pattern show
　Of pure primeval love.

　　Giver of concord, Prince of peace,
　　　Meek, lamb-like Son of God,
　　Bid our unruly passions cease;
　　　Oh quench them with Thy blood.

　　Us into closest union draw,
　　　And in our inward parts
　　Let kindness sweetly write her law;
　　　Let love command our hearts.

　　Saviour, look down with pitying eyes;
　　　Our jarring wills control.
　　Let cordial, kind affections rise
　　　And harmonize the soul.

　　Oh let us find the ancient way
　　　Our wondering foes to move,
　　And force the heathen world to say,
　　　'See how these Christians love!'

　　　No, they cry, it cannot be;
　　　Christians never will agree!
　　　All the world Thy word deny,
　　　Yet we on the truth rely,

THE LIFE OF THE CHURCH

Sure, in that appointed day,
Thou wilt give us all one way,
Show us each to other joined,
One in heart and one in mind.

Hasten then the general peace;
Bid Thy people's discord cease.
All united in Thy name,
Let us think and speak the same.
Then the world shall know and own
God Himself hath made us one,
Thee their Lord with us embrace,
Sing thine everlasting praise.

JESU, great Shepherd of the sheep,
　　To Thee for help we fly;
Thy little flock in safety keep,
　　For oh the wolf is nigh.

Us into Thy protection take,
　　And gather with Thine arm;
Unless the fold we first forsake,
　　The wolf can never harm.

We laugh to scorn his cruel power,
　　While at our Shepherd's side;
The sheep he never can devour,
　　Unless he first divide.

Oh do not suffer him to part
　　The souls that here agree;
But make us of one mind and heart,
　　And keep us one in Thee.

JESUS, Thee the Head we own,
　　The Saviour of mankind.
Thou of twain hast made us one,
　　Hast souls divided joined.

PRAYERS FOR THE CHURCH

We Thy mystic body are;
In Thee the scattered members meet—
Through Thine all-prevailing prayer
Our harmony complete

By one Spirit inspired and led,
We to each other cleave;
Nourished with immortal Bread,
The life of faith we live;
Called to purity and peace
The fellowship of saints we prove
In the bond of perfectness
And unity of love.

In Thy heavenly Father one,
We all His children are;
Of Thy flesh and of Thy bone,
Thy holy nature share;
All into Thy Spirit drink,
All baptized into Thy name,
One in heart and mind, we think
And act and speak the same.

Closer knit to God and Thee,
Jesus in us make known
All the hidden mystery,
The Holy Three in One;
Thus convinced, the world shall feel
Thy Father's gracious will and mind,
Know He sent Thee down to dwell
In us and all mankind.

UNCHANGEABLE, Almighty Lord,
Our souls upon Thy truth we stay;
Accomplish now Thy faithful word,
And give, oh give us all one way.

Oh let us all join hand in hand
Who seek redemption in Thy blood,
Fast in one mind and spirit stand,
And build the temple of our God.

THE LIFE OF THE CHURCH

Giver of peace and unity,
　Send down Thy mild pacific Dove;
We all shall then in one agree
　And breathe the Spirit of Thy love.

We all shall think and speak the same
　Delightful lesson of Thy grace,
One undivided Christ proclaim,
　And jointly glory in Thy praise.

Regard Thine own eternal prayer
　And send a peaceful answer down.
To us Thy Father's name declare;
　Unite and perfect us in one.

So shall the world believe and know
　That God hath sent Thee from above,
When Thou art seen in us below,
　And every soul displays Thy love.

　　Jesus, with Thy Father come,
　　　And bring our inward Guide;
　　Make our hearts Thy humble home,
　　　And in Thy house abide;
　　Show us with Thy presence filled,
　Filled with glory from Thy throne,
　　Wholly sanctified and sealed
　　　And perfected in one.

　　Thus Thy Father's kind intent
　　　Let the whole world perceive,
　　Know He from His bosom sent
　　　His Son that all may live,
　　Sent Thee every soul to bless,
　That in Thy loving Spirit joined
　　All may with one mouth confess
　　　The Saviour of mankind.

PRAYERS FOR THE CHURCH

FOR THE WORK OF EVANGELISM

MAKE our earthly souls a field
Which God delights to bless;
Let us in due season yield
The fruits of righteousness;
Make us trees of paradise
Which more and more Thy grace may show,
Deeper sink, and higher rise,
And to perfection grow.

Let our leaves the nations heal;
Our fruits a blessing make.
Let the world our influence feel,
Our gospel-grace partake;
Grace to help in time of need
Pour out on sinners from above;
All Thy Spirit's fulness shed
In showers of heavenly love.

THE WORLD's bright Day did then appear,
When present in His body here
Our Lord vouchsafed to shine;
His heavenly life and doctrine showed
The majesty of real God,
The eternal Light divine.

But present in Thy Spirit still,
Jesus, Thou dost Thyself reveal
In this Thy Church below;
And every soul, though wrapped in night,
May see Thine all enlivening light
And Thee his Saviour know.

Light of the world, appear to all,
To raise the nations from their fall
Thy glorious beams impart.
Their sin and ignorance disperse,
And cheer Thy gladdened universe,
And shine in every heart.

THE LIFE OF THE CHURCH

FATHER of me, and all mankind,
   And all the hosts above,
Let every understanding mind
   Unite to praise Thy love,
To know Thy nature and Thy name,
   One God in Persons three,
And glorify the great I AM
   Through all eternity.

Thy peace and joy and righteousness
   In all our bosoms reign.
Thy kingdom come, with power and grace,
   To every heart of man,
The kingdom of established peace
   Which can no more remove,
The perfect power of godliness,
   The omnipotence of love.

Hasten that happiest gospel-day,
   When all on earth, forgiven,
As fully shall Thy will obey
   As angels do in heaven;
While not one disharmonious string
   Is heard below, above,
But all in perfect concert sing,
   And praise the God we love.

THE NAME be known from east to west,
The truth and power and love confessed
   Of Christ, our great exalted Lord.
Jesus, we long Thy day to see,
To hail Thy sovereign Majesty
   By all the heathen world adored.

The only God supreme Thou art;
To Thee may every praying heart
   Present itself an offering pure,
And let our whole converted race,
Who taste Thy love and sing Thy praise,
   To all eternity endure.

PRAYERS FOR THE CHURCH

God, on us Thy grace bestow,
  Thy freely-pardoning grace;
Bless us from our sins, and show
  The brightness of Thy face.
Let Thy way on earth be shown;
  Thee let every sinner find;
Make Thy great salvation known
  To us and all mankind.

Let the people praise Thee, Lord,
  The God of truth and grace;
Thee, the everlasting Word,
  Let all the people praise.
O give thanks, rejoice and sing,
  Every creature under heaven;
Let them triumph in their King
  And shout their sins forgiven.

Thou shalt judge the nations right,
  Thy equal sway maintain,
Rule them by Thy mercy's might
  And bless them by Thy reign.
Let the people praise Thee, Lord,
  Thee, the God of truth and grace.
Thee, the everlasting Word,
  Let all the nations praise.

Then in perfect holiness
  The earth her fruit shall have;
God, our God, His saints shall bless
  And to the utmost save.
God shall perfect us in one;
  Then the world their Lord shall see,
Thee the nations all shall own
  And give their hearts to Thee.

THE LIFE OF THE CHURCH

YE KINGDOMS of the earth, arise.
Sing unto God who bows the skies;
　Salute the almighty King of kings.
He from the heaven of heavens comes down,
Forsakes His everlasting throne,
　And grace and peace to sinners brings.

Hear Him, ye nations, and rejoice;
His voice He sends, His mighty voice,
　And bids you come to Him and live.
Sinners, receive the gospel word;
Your loving, all-redeeming Lord
　With joy let all mankind receive.

Thee, by the highest heavens adored,
Tremendous, everlasting Lord,
　The God of Israel we proclaim.
The glory of Thy grace receive;
All blessing, might, and thanks we give,
　All praise and love, to Jesu's name.

SERVANT of God and Son of Man,
　Eternal Son of God most high,
Fulfil the great redeeming plan
　Which brought Thee, Saviour, from the sky,
Anointed by His Spirit, and sealed,
With all His glorious fulness filled.

Discouraged at our wayward ways,
　We trust Thee, that Thou wilt not fail,
But carry on Thy work of grace
　Till mercy over sin prevail,
And fix on earth Thy righteous throne,
And reign in all our hearts alone.

Oh may the power of love proceed
　With Thee into the souls of men.
Throughout the world Thy gospel spread;
　And let Thy glorious Spirit reign,
On all the ransomed race bestowed,
And fill the universe with God.

PRAYERS FOR THE CHURCH

FOR THE COMPLETING OF THE CHURCH

ONE GOD the children all confess,
    One Head the members all adore,
One Spirit of faith and holiness
    Who fills them with His love and power;
One flock, one body, and one bride,
    So closely joined in mind and heart,
That neither earth nor hell divide,
    That neither life nor death can part.

Yet multitudes uncalled remain,
    Wide wandering in the wilderness;
Thee, Saviour, let Thy love constrain
    To bring in every sheep that strays.
Oh let them hear and flock to Thee
    From north and south and east and west,
Together all Thy glory see
    And in their Shepherd's bosom rest.

The secret whisper of Thy love,
    The small still voice, shall bring them home,
Though far as hell from heaven they rove
    From God, they to Thy Church shall come.
For Thy own gracious promise sake
    Thou wilt incline their hearts to obey,
One undivided people make,
    And give us all one perfect way.

Then jarring sentiments shall cease
    And discord's voice be heard no more,
While in the truth of holiness
    Thy Church with one consent adore;
Flesh of Thy flesh, bone of Thy bone,
    The members each to each shall join,
Cemented by Thy blood alone,
    And one with unity divine.

THE LIFE OF THE CHURCH

JESUS, we wait to see
That spotless Church of Thine,
The heaven-appointed ministry,
The hierarchy divine.
Command her now to rise
With perfect beauty pure,
Long as the new-made earth and skies
To flourish and endure;

A Church which may remain,
With all Thy works restored,
Commensurate with time, and gain
The nature of her Lord;
A Church to comprehend
The whole wide human race,
And live in joys that never end
Before Thy glorious face.

FOR THE PERFECTING OF THE CHURCH

COLLECTED, perfected in one,
Jesus, Thy sinless people show,
And through the wondering world make known
Thy glorious, spotless Church below.

Oh may I on her glories gaze,
Her glories all to me be given,
When God vouchsafes to sound her praise
And spread her fame through earth and heaven.

PRAYERS FOR USE BY SERVANTS OF THE CHURCH

FOR A CHORISTER

THOU God of harmony and love,
Whose name transports the saints above
   And lulls the ravished spheres,
On Thee in feeble strains I call,
And mix my humble voice with all
   Thy heavenly choristers.

If well I know the tuneful art
To captivate a human heart,
   The glory, Lord, be Thine;
A servant of Thy blessed will,
I here devote my utmost skill
   To sound the praise divine.

Thine own musician, Lord, inspire,
And let my consecrated lyre
   Repeat the psalmist's part;
His Son and Thine reveal in me,
And fill with sacred melody
   The fibres of my heart.

Oh may I with Thy saints aspire,
The meanest of that dazzling choir
   Who chant Thy praise above;
Mixed with the bright musician-band,
May I a heavenly minstrel stand,
   And sing the song of love.

THE LIFE OF THE CHURCH

FOR A PHYSICIAN

PHYSICIAN, Friend of human kind,
Whose pitying love is pleased to find
  A cure for every ill,
By Thee raised up, by Thee bestowed
To do my fellow-creatures good,
  I come to serve Thy will.

Confiding in Thy name alone,
Jesus, I in Thy work go on,
  To tend Thy sick and poor.
Dispenser of Thy medicines I;
But Thou the blessing must supply,
  But Thou must give the cure.

FOR TEACHERS AND LEADERS

SHEPHERDS the sheep should feed
When Jesus gives the word,
Whose grace provides with all they need
The followers of their Lord.
  God will Himself supply
  The impotence of man,
And do, poor souls to satisfy,
All that the Almighty can.

Jesus doth not enjoin
Impossibilities,
But shows our need of grace divine
The Lord our God to please;
  The things within our power
  Commands us to fulfil,
Employ His grace, and ask for more
To do His perfect will.

For what Thou didst bestow
Thy love we glorify,
But own we can no farther go
Without a fresh supply.

PRAYERS FOR USE BY SERVANTS OF THE CHURCH

We every word receive
Our Lord vouchsafes to say;
Command whate'er Thou wilt, but give
Thy servants power to obey.

FOR PREACHERS

MY HEAVENLY Lord, I would from Thee
The double grace receive:
With true Divine simplicity
The gospel preach and live,
Inform the souls whose good I seek
And do the Christian part,
Words to the understanding speak
But actions to the heart.

REJOICE, ye followers of your Lord,
Who preach the pure, pacific word;
Disturbers of the public peace,
Troublers of sleeping consciences,
As enemies to Church and State,
Whom all men persecute and hate,
To you your Master's cup is given
And great is your reward in heaven.

LET ALL who speak in Jesu's name
To Him submit their every word,
Implicit faith in them disclaim
And send the hearers to their Lord,
Who doth His Father's will reveal,
The only Guide infallible.

THE LIFE OF THE CHURCH

Jesus, to me Thy mind impart,
  Be Thou Thine own Interpreter;
Explain the Scripture to my heart,
  That when the Church Thy servant hear,
Taught by the oracles divine,
They all may own the word is Thine.

JESUS, Thy servants bless,
  Who sent by Thee proclaim
The peace and joy and righteousness
  Experienced in Thy name,
The kingdom of our God
  Which Thy great Spirit imparts,
The power of thy victorious blood
  Which reigns in faithful hearts.

Our souls with faith supply,
  With life and liberty;
And lo, we preach and testify
  The things concerning Thee.
We live for this alone,
  Thy grace to minister,
And all Thou hast for sinners done
  In life and death declare.

JESUS, my strength and righteousness,
  My Saviour and my King,
Triumphantly Thy name I bless,
  Thy conquering name I sing.

Thou gavest me to speak Thy word
  In the appointed hour,
I have proclaimed my dying Lord
  And felt Thy Spirit's power.

Oh let me have Thy presence still;
  Set as a flint my face,
To show the counsel of Thy will,
  Which saves a world by grace.

PRAYERS FOR USE BY SERVANTS OF THE CHURCH

FOR A CANDIDATE FOR THE MINISTRY

MEANEST of all who Thee confess,
The least of all Thy witnesses,
Oh that I may be counted meet
To wash Thy dear disciples' feet.

This, only this, do I require
(Thou know'st 'tis all my heart's desire):
Freely what I receive to give,
The servant of Thy Church to live,

After my lowly Lord to go
And wait upon Thy saints below,
Enjoy the grace to angels given
And serve the royal heirs of heaven.

FOR ORDINANDS

I THANK Thee, Lord of earth and heaven,
That Thou to me, e'en me, hast given
    The knowledge of Thy grace
(Which flesh and blood could ne'er reveal)
And called a babe Thy love to tell
    And stammer out Thy praise.

Thy Spirit send me from above,
Spirit of meek long-suffering love,
    Of all-sufficient grace;
Endue me with Thy constant mind,
So good, so obstinately kind
    To our rebellious race.

Be this my whole employ below,
Before Thy little flock to go
    And in Thy steps to tread;
Shepherd of souls, I fain would be
Their faithful pastor under Thee,
    And feed as I am fed.

THE LIFE OF THE CHURCH

Master, Thy promised help I claim,
Sent forth to testify Thy name
  Which speaks a world forgiven,
Sent forth Thy mercy to display,
And teach, as taught of Thee, the way,
  The living way to heaven.

Thy servant in the gospel, I
For all my fellow-servants cry
  In never ceasing prayer:
By us in each hard trial stand,
Support us with Thine outstretched hand,
  And all our burdens bear.

O ALL-ATONING Lamb,
  O Saviour of mankind,
If every soul may in Thy name
  With me salvation find,
If Thou hast chosen me
  To testify Thy grace
(That vast unfathomable sea
  Which covers all our race),

Equip me for the war
  And teach my hands to fight,
My simple upright heart prepare
  And guide my words aright.
Control my every thought;
  My every sin remove;
Let all my works in Thee be wrought,
Let all be wrought in love.

Oh arm me with the mind,
  Meek Lamb, that was in Thee,
And let my knowing zeal be joined
  To perfect charity;
With calm and tempered zeal
  Let me enforce Thy call,
And vindicate Thy gracious will,
  Which offers life to all.

PRAYERS FOR USE BY SERVANTS OF THE CHURCH

Oh may I love like Thee
    And in Thy footsteps tread;
Thou hatest all iniquity,
    But nothing Thou hast made.
Oh may I learn Thy art
    With meekness to reprove,
To hate the sin with all my heart
    But still the sinner love.

Oh do not let me trust
    In any arm but Thine;
Humble, oh humble to the dust
    This stubborn soul of mine.
Cast all my reeds aside,
    Captivate every thought;
And drain me of my strength and pride,
    And bring me down to nought.

Thou dost not stand in need
    Of me to prop Thy cause,
To assert Thy general grace or spread
    The victory of Thy cross.
Yet Thou dost me command;
    I answer to Thy call,
A witness of Thy grace I stand,
    Thy grace which is for all.

FOR MINISTERS

EVERY gospel-minister
    All his gifts from Christ receives;
Nothing has he to confer
    But what first to him He gives.
Christ it is who breaks the bread,
    Gives the word by faith applied;
Then the multitude is fed,
    Then their souls are satisfied.

THE LIFE OF THE CHURCH

Who on Providence depend
  Fear no insufficiency,
All their stock for Jesus spend,
  All His followers' wants supply.
Can a stock exhausted be,
  Still replenished from above?
Jesus is their Treasury,
  Truth divine, and Power, and Love.

THY CALL, O God, to man conveys
Sufficiency of gifts and grace;
Wherefore to me Thy Spirit impart,
And bless me with a pastor's heart;
The servant of Thy people I
Shall then rejoice to live and die.

JESUS, from whom all blessings flow,
Great Builder of Thy Church below;
If now Thy Spirit moves my breast,
Hear, and fulfil Thine own request.

Feed and protect Thy little flock,
Under the shadow of their Rock—
The holy seed, the royal race,
The standing monuments of Thy grace.

Oh let them all Thy mind express,
Stand forth Thy chosen witnesses,
Thy power unto salvation show
And perfect holiness below.

Oh make them of one soul and heart,
The all-conforming mind impart,
Spirit of peace and unity,
The sinless mind that was in Thee.

PRAYERS FOR USE BY SERVANTS OF THE CHURCH

From every sinful wrinkle free,
Redeemed from all iniquity,
The fellowship of saints make known,
And, O my God, may I be one.

SHEPHERD of souls, the great, the good,
For the dear purchase of Thy blood
    To Thee in faith we pray:
The lambs and sheep within Thy fold,
Now in Thy book of life enrolled,
    Preserve unto that day.

Whom Thou by us hast gathered in,
Defend the little flock from sin,
    From error's paths secure;
Stay with them, Lord, when we depart,
And guard the issues of their heart,
    And keep their conscience pure.

What then can their protection be?
The virtue that proceeds from Thee,
    The power of humble love.
The strength of all-sufficient grace,
Received in Thine appointed ways,
    Can bring them safe above.

Now, Saviour, clothe them with Thy power,
And arm their souls against that hour
    With faith invincible;
Teach them to wield the Spirit's sword,
And mighty in the written word
    To rout both earth and hell.

When I, from all my burdens freed,
Am numbered with the peaceful dead
    In everlasting rest,
Pity the sheep I leave behind;
My God, unutterably kind,
    And lodge them in Thy breast.

THE LIFE OF THE CHURCH

Ah never suffer them to leave
The Church, where Thou art pleased to give
  Such tokens of Thy grace.
Confirm them in their calling here,
Till ripe by holiest love to appear
  Before Thy glorious face.

Whom I into Thy hands commend,
Wilt Thou not keep them to the end,
  Thou infinite in love?
Assure me, Lord, it shall be so,
And let my quiet spirit go
  To join the Church above.

FORTH in Thy strength, O Lord, I go
  Thy Gospel to proclaim,
Thy sovereign righteousness to show,
  And glorify Thy name.

Ordained I am, and sent by Thee
  As by the Father Thou.
And lo, Thou always art with me;
  I plead the promise now.

Oh give me now to speak Thy word
  In this appointed hour;
Attend it with Thy Spirit, Lord,
  And let it come with power.

Open the hearts of all that hear,
  To make their Saviour room;
Now let them find redemption near,
  Let faith by hearing come.

Give them to hear the word as Thine,
  And (while they thus receive)
Prove it the saving power divine
  To sinners that believe.

PRAYERS FOR USE BY SERVANTS OF THE CHURCH

FOR AN AGED MINISTER BEFORE PREACHING

GUARDIAN of my hoary hairs,
   Let me still dispense Thy grace
(Meanest of Thy messengers,
   Ready to conclude my race),
Still Thy promised presence prove,
Still proclaim Thy pardoning love.

Touch my lips with hallowing fire;
   Utterance let Thy Spirit give;
Fill my heart with pure desire
   That a dying world may live,
Witnesses of sins forgiven,
Sons of God and heirs of heaven.

Open now the gospel door;
   Now the gospel truths reveal;
Clothe Thy word with secret power,
   Saving, irresistible,
Power that life divine imparts,
Breaks and heals attentive hearts.

Faith which sweetly works by love
   Let it now by hearing come,
That begotten from above
   Souls may languish after home,
Spotless in Thine image rise,
Grasp through death the immortal prize.

Crown of my rejoicing, Lord,
   Let me there my children meet,
Saved by the engrafted word,
   Singing round Thy glorious seat;
Children of my faith and prayer,
Let me die to meet them there.

THE LIFE OF THE CHURCH

Instrument of saving them,
    Jesus, claim me for Thine own,
That I may in bliss supreme
    Cast my crown before Thy throne,
Face to face my Saviour see,
Gaze through all eternity.

The Daily Round

THE CIRCUMSTANCES OF LIFE

ON A BIRTHDAY

GREAT Author of my being,
   Thankful I bow before Thee;
     Thine own I am
     From whom I came,
   And all my powers adore Thee.

I triumph in existence,
   Enjoy my Maker's favour,
     Created I
     To glorify
   And love my God for ever.

IN A HURRY OF BUSINESS

HELP, Lord! The busy foe
   Is as a flood come in.
Lift up Thy standard, and o'erthrow
   This soul-distracting sin.
   This sudden tide of care
   Stem by that bloody tree,
Nor let the rising torrent bear
   My soul away from Thee.

The praying spirit breathe;
   The watching power impart;
From all entanglements beneath
   Call off my anxious heart.
   My feeble mind sustain,
   By worldly thoughts oppressed;
Appear, and bid me turn again
   To my eternal rest.

THE DAILY ROUND

Swift to my rescue come;
Thine own this moment seize;
Gather my wandering spirit home
And keep in perfect peace.
Suffered no more to rove
O'er all the earth abroad,
Arrest the prisoner of Thy love
And shut me up in God.

IN UNCERTAINTY

To WHAT am I reserved? Great God,
  The counsel of Thy will display;
Nor let me underneath the load
  Of anxious doubt for ever stay.

Thou seest I cannot journey on,
  Till Thou the lingering cloud remove
And make the destined action known
  And lead me by the fire of love.

My every choice, desire, design,
  I now implicitly submit;
My will is fixed to follow Thine,
  And lies indifferent at Thy feet.

Thy wisdom and Thy power shall join
  To effectuate what Thy love decrees,
My work and place and friends assign,
  And crown the whole with full success.

Jesus, my faithful Guide,
  For Thy advice I stay,
Who wilt not let me wander wide
  Of my appointed way.

THE CIRCUMSTANCES OF LIFE

Till Thou reveal Thy will,
In calm uncertainty,
I know not what to do, but still
Mine eyes are fixed on Thee.

Till Thou direction send,
Delightfully resigned
I mark the openings, and attend
The tokens of Thy mind;
What Thou wouldst have me do
By plainest signs to prove
I wait, and step by step pursue
The leadings of Thy love.

IN DANGER

MORE than a host of angels,
Thy promise to deliver
Comforts our hearts,
And strength imparts,
And life that lasts for ever.

IN THREAT OF WAR

WITH lowly reverential joy
Thy mercy we embrace,
This solemn interval employ
In ceaseless prayer and praise.

Whate'er these threatening wars portend,
Whate'er Thy will decrees,
Our souls that on Thy love depend
Are kept in perfect peace.

Who rest beneath the Almighty's wings
May cast their cares away;
Whate'er event to-morrow brings,
We live for God to-day.

THE DAILY ROUND

IN PAIN

Thou Lamb of God, Thou Prince of peace,
　　For Thee my thirsty soul doth pine.
My longing soul implores Thy grace;
　　Oh make in me Thy likeness shine.

With fraudless, even, humble mind,
　　Thy will in all things may I see;
In love be every wish resigned,
　　And hallowed my whole heart to Thee.

When pain o'er my weak flesh prevails,
　　With lamb-like patience arm my breast;
When grief my wounded soul assails,
　　In lowly meekness may I rest.

Close by Thy side still may I keep,
　　Howe'er life's various current flow,
With steadfast eye mark every step
　　And follow Thee where'er Thou go.

Thou, Lord, the dreadful fight hast won;
　　Alone Thou hast the wine-press trod.
In me Thy strengthening grace be shown;
　　Oh may I conquer through Thy blood.

So when on Sion Thou shalt stand,
　　And all heaven's host adore their King,
Shall I be found at Thy right hand,
　　And free from pain Thy glories sing.

This pain, this consecrated pain,
　　With which my soul and flesh are filled,
Thy instrument if Thou ordain,
　　The pure and perfect love shall yield;
But by whatever means 'tis done,
The work and praise is all Thine own.

THE CIRCUMSTANCES OF LIFE

IN SICKNESS

HAIL, great Physician of mankind!
    Saviour Thou art from every ill.
Health in Thy name alone we find;
    Thy name doth in the medicine heal.

Thy name the fainting soul restores,
    Strength to the wearied body brings,
Renews exhausted nature's powers,
    And bears us as on eagle's wings.

Faith in Thy sovereign name I have
    And wait its healing power to know,
Assured that it my flesh shall save
    Till all Thy work is done below.

Then, Saviour, for my spirit call,
    My spirit all conformed to Thine;
And let this tabernacle fall,
    To rise rebuilt by hands divine.

IN OLD AGE

I TOO, forewarned by Jesu's love,
    Must shortly lay my body down;
But ere my soul from earth remove,
    Oh let me put Thine image on.

Saviour, Thy meek and lowly mind
    Be to Thine aged servant given,
And glad I'll drop this tent, to find
    My everlasting house in heaven.

THE DAILY ROUND

PREPARING FOR DEATH

Jesus, the just, the good,
Remember Calvary,
And claim the purchase of Thy blood,
Expended all for me.
Not my own faithfulness,
But Thine I humbly plead,
Who wilt not quench a spark of grace,
Nor break a bruised reed.

I ask not ecstasies;
But with a loving heart,
In steadfast hope and humble peace
Permit me to depart.
Suffice that here I know
My sins through grace forgiven,
And calmly blessed, with safety go
To endless joys in heaven.

Of all our bliss the fount and root,
The tree, the blossom, and the fruit
   Is immortality;
Fulness of joy Thy presence gives,
And heaven its heavenliness receives,
   When Thee unveiled we see.

My immortality Thou art;
The glorious earnest in my heart,
   Jesus, to me be given;
Of Thee possessed, I ask no more,
But happy in Thy love adore
   The joy of earth and heaven.

While I this adoration give,
Thou wilt transport my soul to live
   And reign with Thee above,
Where faith is sweetly lost in sight,
And hope in full supreme delight
   And everlasting love.

THE CIRCUMSTANCES OF LIFE

WARNED from the body to depart,
  What shall I of my God desire?
Pardon and grace to keep my heart
  Till Thou my ready soul require.

All that is past, my God, forgive;
  For the short time to come defend;
And strengthening without sin to live,
  Oh bless me with a peaceful end.

Meet for the fellowship above,
  The glories of eternity,
Thy servant, Lord, with ease remove,
  And let me fall asleep in Thee.

Do Thou, if so Thy love ordain,
  Gently the knot of life untie;
And free from sin, and free from pain,
  In mercy's arms I sweetly die.

UNNUMBERED deaths and snares
  Thy love hath turned aside;
And still, O God, to hoary hairs
  Thou art my faithful Guide.
Thy miracles of grace
  Thou daily dost renew,
Straighten the inextricable maze
  And bring me strangely through.

Why then am I cast down,
  With anxious thoughts oppressed,
With doubts if Thou wilt lead me on
  To my eternal rest?
Thy will and power are joined
  The helpless to defend;
And saved so long, I trust to find
  Salvation in my end.

THE DAILY ROUND

Confiding in Thy word,
I ask the grace unknown;
According to Thy promise, Lord,
Let it in me be done.
My faith's defects supply,
Almighty to forgive,
And then I get me up and die,
And then for ever live.

ENMITY

WHEN ACCUSED OF EVIL

WHEN He could Himself defend,
The Saviour holds His peace,
Our apologies to end
And clamours to suppress.
Hear we then the speechless Lamb
Who doth our eagerness reprove,
Silence and for ever shame
Our self-excusing love.

WHEN SUFFERING ENMITY

AGAINST the instrument of ill
Oh may I no resentment find,
No wrong, vindictive temper feel,
Unfriendly wish, or thought unkind;
But put the deep compassion on,
The tender mercy of Thy Son.

Still would I keep the Lamb in view,
Harmless in thought, and word, and deed,
That Lover of His foes pursue
Who suffered in His murderers' stead,
Expired Himself that they might live,
And meekly gasped in death, 'Forgive.'

ENMITY

His Spirit into my soul inspire,
   That in true holiness renewed,
With pure, benevolent desire,
   For evil I may render good,
Kind to my adversary prove
And cruel hate requite with love.

If Thou forgive my debt immense,
   I may forgive a trivial debt,
A fellow-servant's hundred pence
   Against ten thousand talents set.
I *do* forgive, myself forgiven,
And haste to meet my foe in heaven.

JESU, Thy legacy I take,
   The pattern Thou hast left behind,
To suffer all things for Thy sake;
   Thy patient, meek, submissive mind
I long throughout my life to express,
And copy all Thy righteousness.

Oh may I with Thy calmness meet
   My destined share of grief and woe,
And meek as Thee the men entreat
   With love, who bitter hatred show,
Only to God their names declare,
And bless them in my dying prayer.

Who hunt my soul with cruel scorn,
   Who hate and vex me without cause,
My bitterest persecutors turn,
   Like those that nailed Thee to Thy cross;
Freely by Thee, by me forgiven,
Oh let me meet my foes in heaven.

THE DAILY ROUND

Me when an enemy to God,
   Thou didst with arms of love embrace;
Though infinite the debt I owed,
   Thy free, immeasurable grace
Forgave; and still Thou daily art
Inscribing pardon on my heart.

Oh that I may like Thee forget
   Whate'er to me my brother owes,
Remit the re-contracted debt,
   A thousand times embrace my foes,
And still forgive with charity
Unbounded as Thy love to me.

My mortal foe, whom for Thy sake,
   Saviour, for Thine alone, I love,
Humbled into Thy favour take;
   Prepare him for a place above;
Call him with me Thy throne to share,
And join us in Thy praises there.

Come, O my soul, the call obey;
   Take up the burden of thy Lord.
His practice is thy living way,
   Thy guide His pure unerring word;
The lovely perfect pattern read,
And haste in all His steps to tread.

Still let me on that Pattern gaze.
   How meek and motionless He stands!
They spit upon His sacred face;
   They buffet with unhallowed hands,
They bow the knee, present the reed,
And mock whom they have doomed to bleed.

ENMITY

Oh may His love my heart constrain,
   My every rising thought control,
Sweeten the cup of grief and pain,
   And melt and meeken all my soul,
Conform me to the Crucified,
My God who for His murderers died.

Love only can the conquest win
   And make me as my lamblike God;
Through love I conquer all their sin,
   And strive, resisting unto blood,
Strive to secure the glorious wreath,
Resisting by enduring death.

Come, O my Jesu, from above;
   Endue me with Thy constant mind.
Inspire me with Thy patient love,
   Thou suffering Saviour of mankind,
My faith increase; my heart prepare;
And arm, and bid me all things bear.

Thy power into my heart inspeak;
   And lo, I come to meet Thy pain,
To turn like Thee the other cheek,
   All wrong and violence to sustain,
Never against my foes to stand,
But sink beneath their bruising hand.

I will not take the proffered sword
   Or stoop to feeble man for aid;
Lead me away with Christ my Lord,
   To scorn or bonds or slaughter lead.
A follower of that silent Lamb,
The man whom now ye seek, I am.

His servant and disciple see,
   Resolved His weal or woe to share;
A Galilean seize in me,
   And let me as my Master fare;
Convict (for I my crime confess)
Of following after righteousness.

THE DAILY ROUND

MY PATTERN in Thy death I see;
 A voice is in Thy streaming blood.
It bids me bear the scourge like Thee,
 Like Thee commit my cause to God,
Like Thee the injurious world oppose,
Like Thee avenge me of my foes.

Thou didst the meek example leave
 That I might in Thy footsteps tread,
Might like the Man of sorrows grieve,
 And groan, and bow with Thee my head,
Thy dying in my body bear,
And all Thy state of passion share.

Saved is the life for Thy sake lost,
 Hidden from earth, but found in Thee;
To suffer is to triumph most,
 And death is immortality.
They who for Thee their all have given
Have nobly bartered earth for heaven.

This is the straight and royal way
 That leads us to the courts above;
Oh let me never from it stray,
 Till on the wings of perfect love
I take my last triumphant flight
From Calvary's to Sion's height.

AFTER STRIFE

REPENTANCE upon both bestow,
Our foes and us, that each may know
 Their sins through faith forgiven,
That all may cordially embrace,
And sweetly reconciled by grace
 Go hand in hand to heaven.

FRIENDSHIP

WHEN VISITING FRIENDS

PEACE be on this house bestowed,
  Peace on all that here reside;
Let the unknown peace of God
  With the man of peace abide.
Let the Spirit now come down;
  Let the blessing now take place;
Son of peace, receive thy crown,
  Fulness of the Gospel grace.

Christ, my Master and my Lord,
  Let me Thy forerunner be.
Oh be mindful of Thy word;
  Visit them, and visit me.
To this house and all herein,
  Now let Thy salvation come;
Save our souls from inbred sin;
  Make them Thine eternal home.

PRAYERS FOR SICK FRIENDS

HUMBLY prostrate at Thy feet,
We our will to Thine submit;
Yet, before Thy will is shown,
Trembling we present our own.

Jesus, evermore the same,
Manifest Thy saving name;
Good Physician from above,
Heal the object of Thy love.

SEE, GRACIOUS Lord, with pitying eyes,
My friend who now a sufferer lies;
Come down in mercy from above,
For sick he is whom Thou dost love.

THE DAILY ROUND

His to Thine own afflictions join;
Accept, exalt, and count them Thine;
Thy passion which remains fulfil,
And suffer in Thy members still.

His sickness feel, endure his pain,
His burden bear, his cross sustain,
Grieve in his griefs and sigh his sighs,
And breathe his wishes to the skies.

Enter his heart, possess him whole,
Inspire and actuate his soul;
Himself no longer let it be
That suffers or that lives—but Thee.

Thyself through sufferings perfect made,
Conform him thus to Thee his Head;
Refine, and raise his virtue higher,
When tried and purified by fire.

So when his eyes behold Thee near,
And Thou, his hidden life, appear,
Bright in Thy likeness shall he shine,
All glorious made, and all divine.

MOST meek and tender-hearted Lamb,
Jesus we call on Thy dear name,
   Nor shall we call in vain;
In Thee we have not a high-priest
Who cannot be like us distressed,
   For Thou Thyself art man.

Thou feelest all the woes we feel;
A sufferer in Thy members still,
   A man of griefs Thou art.
And now Thou dost the sickness bear
Of him for whom we make our prayer
   And pour out all our heart.

FRIENDSHIP

Still, gracious Lord, delight to shed
Thy blessings on his favoured head;
   Thy choicest blessings shower.
Preserve his mind in perfect peace;
And when his sufferings most increase,
   Oh let his joys be more.

Give him Thy meek and quiet mind;
Patient, and perfectly resigned
   Oh make his humble heart.
Jesu, approach, and touch his hand
(We ask in faith) and now command
   The fever to depart.

ON THE DEATH OF A FRIEND

IF DEATH my friend and me divide,
Thou dost not, Lord, my sorrow chide,
   Or frown my tears to see;
Restrained from passionate excess,
Thou bidd'st me mourn in calm distress
   For them that rest in Thee.

I feel a strong immortal hope,
Which bears my mournful spirit up
   Beneath its mountain-load.
Redeemed from death and grief and pain,
I soon shall find my friend again
   Within the arms of God.

FAMILY LIFE

GRACE BEFORE MEAT

GLORY, love, and praise, and honour
   For our food
   Now bestowed
Render we the Donor.

THE DAILY ROUND

Bounteous God, we now confess Thee;
  God, who thus
  Blessest us,
Meet it is to bless Thee.

THANKFUL for our every blessing,
  Let us sing
  Christ the Spring,
Never, never ceasing.
Source of all our gifts and graces
  Christ we own;
  Christ alone
Calls for all our praises.

He dispels our sin and sadness,
  Life imparts,
  Cheers our hearts,
Fills with food and gladness.
Who Himself for all hath given,
  Us He feeds,
  Us He leads
To a feast in heaven.

MARRIAGE

OUR FRIENDSHIP sanctify and guide;
Unmixed with selfishness and pride,
  Thy glory be our single aim.
In all our fellowship below,
Still let us in Thy footsteps go;
  Let all be done in Thy great name.

Fix on Thyself our single eye;
Oh may we on Thyself rely
  For all the help which each conveys,
The help as from Thy hands receive,
And still to Thee all glory give,
  All thanks, all might, all love, all praise.

FAMILY LIFE

Whate'er Thou dost on one bestow,
Let each the doubled blessing know,
   Let each the common burden bear,
In comforts and in griefs agree,
And wrestle for his friend with Thee
   In all the omnipotence of prayer.

Our mutual prayer accept and seal;
In both Thy glorious self reveal,
   Both with the fire of love baptize.
Thy kingdom in our souls restore,
And keep till we can sin no more,
   Till both in all Thy image rise.

Witnesses of the all-cleansing blood,
Long may we work the works of God
   And do Thy will like those above,
Together spread the gospel sound,
And scatter peace on all around,
   And joy and happiness and love.

And if it be Thy sovereign will,
Jesus, our hearts' desire fulfil:
   When we have run our earthly race,
Let both at once our souls resign
Into those gracious hands of Thine,
   And see at once Thy glorious face.

ON THE BIRTH OF A CHILD

FATHER, Son, and Spirit, come,
   Enter now Thy human shrine.
Take my offspring from the womb;
   Mine he is not, Lord, but Thine.
Thine this moment let him be,
Thine to all eternity.

THE DAILY ROUND

FATHER of all, by whom we are,
   For whom was made whatever is,
Who hast entrusted to our care
   A candidate for glorious bliss,
Poor souls of earth, for help we cry,
   For grace to guard what grace hath given;
We ask the wisdom from on high
   To train our infant up for heaven.

FATHER, instruct my docile heart;
   Apt to instruct I then shall be.
I then shall all Thy words impart,
   And teach (as taught myself by Thee)
My children in their earliest days
To know and live the life of grace.

PARENTS' PRAYERS FOR THEIR CHILDREN

SAVIOUR, I joyfully agree
That children should be brought to Thee;
Myself their infant weakness bear,
And bring them in the arms of prayer.

Hear, Jesus, hear their helpless cry,
Whom now I place beneath Thine eye;
Into Thy kind embraces take,
And subjects of Thy kingdom make.

Thy hand beneficent extend
To bless, and shelter, and defend;
Thy Spirit to my children give
And let them to Thy glory live.

Still let them in Thy footsteps tread,
Till by Thy loving Spirit led
They find the final blessing given,
And triumph with Thy flock in heaven.

FAMILY LIFE

Come, Father, Son, and Holy Ghost,
    To whom we for our children cry.
The good desired and wanted most
    Out of Thy richest grace supply;
The sacred discipline be given,
To train and bring them up for heaven.

Error and ignorance remove,
    Their blindness both of heart and mind;
Give them the wisdom from above,
    Spotless and peaceable and kind;
In knowledge pure their mind renew,
And store with thoughts divinely true.

Learning's redundant part and vain
    Be all cut off and cast aside;
But let them, Lord, the substance gain,
    In every solid truth abide;
Swiftly acquire, and ne'er forego
The knowledge fit for man to know.

Unite the pair so long disjoined,
    Knowledge and vital piety;
Learning and holiness combined,
    And truth and love, let all men see
In these whom up to Thee we give,
Thine, wholly Thine, to die and live.

The children in their earliest days
    To Jesus brought are truly blessed.
He folds them in His kind embrace;
    He warms them in His tender breast.

Our precious child before Thee see,
    And him into Thy arms receive;
Brought by his parents' prayers to Thee,
    Oh may he in Thy kingdom live.

THE DAILY ROUND

We know that Thou art good indeed
   And wouldst to all Thy grace impart;
Put then Thy hands upon his head,
   Put faith into his simple heart.

Thee may he for his portion choose,
   To Thee through life obedient prove,
And now obtain, and never lose,
   The blessing of his Saviour's love.

PRAYER FOR A SICK CHILD

Sleep that soothingly restores
Weary nature's wasted powers,
Gift of an indulgent God,
Be it on our child bestowed.

Jesus, Lord, we cry to Thee,
Friend of helpless infancy;
Now the sufferer's grief suspend,
Now the healing blessing send.

In the arms of faith and prayer
Whom to Thee we humbly bear
Safe in Thy protection keep;
Let him on Thy bosom sleep.

Touched Thyself with human pain,
Sympathizing Son of Man,
Ease the anguish of his breast;
Lull him in Thy arms to rest.

Him we to Thy grace commend,
Confident Thou wilt defend,
Till the answered prayer is sealed,
Till the child of faith is healed.

FAMILY LIFE

A FATHER'S EVENING PRAYER

God, be mercifully near,
Object of a father's fear;
Me into Thy favour take,
Me preserve for Jesu's sake.

With Thy kind protection blessed,
Calm I lay me down to rest;
All I have to Thee resign,
Lodge them in the arms divine.

Her, my dearest earthly friend,
To Thy guardian love commend:
Day and night her Keeper be;
Knit her simple heart to Thee.

Make the little ones Thy care;
Bear them, in Thy bosom bear;
Marked with the Good Shepherd's sign,
Keep my lambs for ever Thine.

PRAYERS FOR MUTUAL LOVE

Come Wisdom, Power, and Grace divine,
Come Jesus, in Thy name to join
   A happy chosen band,
Who fain would prove Thine utmost will,
And all Thy righteous laws fulfil
   In love's benign command.

If pure essential love Thou art,
Thy nature into every heart,
   Thy loving self, inspire,
Bid all our simple souls be one,
United in a bond unknown,
   Baptized with heavenly fire.

THE DAILY ROUND

Supply what every member wants
To found the fellowship of saints;
  Thy Spirit, Lord, supply.
So shall we all Thy love receive,
Together to Thy glory live,
  And to Thy glory die.

Jesu, Lord, we look to Thee.
Let us in Thy name agree;
Show Thyself the Prince of peace;
Bid our discord ever cease.

By Thy reconciling love
Every stumbling-block remove,
Each to each unite, endear;
Come, and spread Thy banner here.

Make us of one heart and mind,
Courteous, pitiful, and kind,
Lowly, meek in thought and word,
Altogether like our Lord.

Let us each for other care,
Each his brother's burden bear,
To the world the pattern give,
Show how true believers live.

Free from anger and from pride,
Let us thus in Thee abide,
All the depth of love express,
All the height of holiness.

Let us then with joy remove
To Thy family above,
On the wings of angels fly,
Show how true believers die.

FAMILY LIFE

A PARENT'S CONFIDENCE IN CHRIST

Who is this condescending Friend
  That doth for children care,
That doth my little ones defend
  And in His bosom bear?

The arms within whose soft embrace
  My sleeping babes I see,
They comprehend unbounded space,
  And grasp infinity.

CHILDREN'S PRAISE

Come, let us our good God proclaim,
  By earth and heaven adored;
Children are bid to praise His name,
  And magnify the Lord.

Let us, with all His saints, agree,
  With all His hosts above;
Part of His family are we,
  His family of love.

And while the angelic army sings,
  With them we humbly join
To extol the glorious King of kings,
  The majesty divine.

Glory to God, and praise, and power,
  Honour and thanks be given;
Children and cherubim adore
  The Lord of earth and heaven.

THE DAILY ROUND

A CHILD'S PRAYER

HOLY Child, of heavenly birth,
God made manifest on earth,
Fain I would Thy follower be,
Live in everything like Thee.

Thy humility impart;
Give me Thy obedient heart,
Free and cheerful to fulfil
All my heavenly Father's will.

Keep me thus to God resigned,
Till His love delights to find
Fairly copied out on me
All the mind which was in Thee.

A WIFE'S PRAYER FOR THE CONVERSION OF HER HUSBAND

SEARCHER of hearts, to Thee I fly,
In doubly deep distress apply
  For help to Thee alone.
I want to feel Thy pardoning love;
I want my husband's heart to prove
  That mystic peace unknown.

Thy goodness formed and turned his mind;
Thou mad'st him generous, just, and kind;
  Yet without Thee he lives.
Thoughtless of all Thy love and care,
His joy, his good, his portion here
  Contented he receives.

Saviour, his slumbering spirit call;
Awake, upraise him from his fall,
  And show the fountain nigh.
Oh give him now himself to see,
To feel his need of faith and Thee,
  And then his need supply.

FAMILY LIFE

Till he awakes I cannot rest,
Or blest myself be singly blest,
　To him so closely joined;
Flesh of his flesh, bone of his bone,
Thyself of twain hast made us one
　In will, and heart, and mind.

Oh may we one become in Thee,
The great mysterious unity
　Of sacred wedlock prove,
To Sion hand in hand repair,
And fitted for Thy presence, share
　The marriage-feast above.

ON THE DEATH OF A MEMBER OF THE FAMILY

TRIUMPHANT soul, the hour is come
　That calls thee to thy Saviour's breast;
The exile is returning home,
　The weary entering into rest;
The angels for their charge attend,
And I must render up my friend.

My friend, how shall I let thee go?
　How can I bear with thee to part?
Dearer than life and all below,
　Wound in the fibres of my heart,
With thee my mingled spirits join;
My life is all wrapped up in thine.

Adieu, dear dying friend, adieu,
　The summons of thy Lord obey;
Mighty and merciful and true,
　He bids thee rise and come away,
With triumph leave this earthly clod
And die into the arms of God.

THE DAILY ROUND

His everlasting arms are spread;
   His faithful mercies never fail;
His hand supports thy sinking head;
   With thee He walks through the dark vale.
He whispers, 'Child, be of good cheer;
Rejoice in death, for I am here.'

Hovering around the new-born heir,
   For thee the shining convoy waits;
To God thy spotless soul they bear.
   Open, ye everlasting gates;
A wide triumphant entrance give,
The glorious new-born heir receive.

Eternal God of truth and grace,
   We magnify Thy faithful love.
We all shall soon behold Thy face;
   We all shall take our seats above;
And we shall in Thy kingdom share,
And we shall meet each other there.

SORROW may enter and remain;
   A Christian heart it should not fill.
Saviour, in us it cannot reign,
   Who bow submissive to Thy will.
Our faith and hope superior rise
   And keep the struggling evil down,
Till fully saved we grasp the prize,
   And through Thy cross obtain Thy crown.

INDEX OF FIRST LINES AND SOURCES

Capital Roman numerals refer to the volumes of the *Poetical Works*, from which all the hymns have been taken.
Arabic numerals refer to the pages of those volumes.
Small Roman numerals refer to verses. (Where no verse numbers are given in the reference to the source, the whole hymn has been used.)
Small *italic letters* refer to lines of verses.
N prefixed to a number indicates that the verse or hymn is so numbered in the *Poetical Works*;
S indicates that the references to which it is prefixed are to the verses and lines of the present selection. The words which follow these references are those of the original text, except that
  Plural means that the pronouns (and the nouns which go with them) which are singular in the present selection are plural in the *Poetical Works*;
  Singular means that such words which are plural in the present selection are singular in the *Poetical Works*;
  First person means that the pronouns which are in the third person in the present selection are in the first person in the *Poetical Works*;
  Second person means that the pronouns which are in the third person in the present selection are in the second person in the *Poetical Works*;
  Third person means that the pronouns which are in the second person in the present selection are in the third person in the *Poetical Works*;
  Editor means that the lines so indicated have been supplied by the editor.
The spelling and punctuation have been brought into line with modern custom, and so has the use of italics and capitals. Occasionally verses have been divided into two or joined together. It has not been thought necessary, however, to record in detail minor changes of such kinds.
All the headings have been supplied by the editor.

Actions He more than words requires . . . 86
 X.204.ii; X.271.*abcdfh*
 S ii.*a*—Conscious from whom
 S ii.*b*—Our faith's
 S ii.*d*—With humble
 S ii.*e*—Show forth the heavenly Giver's
A follower of Thy patient Son 60
 X.404.N682; XIII.83–4.i, iii; XII.82.iii
 S ii.*c*—While every true
 S iii.*b*—Resign'd, through life I
 S iv.*a*—on Thee we fix our eyes
 S iv.*f*—our full salvation

INDEX OF FIRST LINES AND SOURCES

Against the instrument of ill 154
   VIII.427
   S i.*e*—the yearning bowels
   S i.*f*—tender mercies
Ah, my dear Lord, whose changeless love. . . 56
   I.131–2.i–ix, xii
All creatures, praise the Eternal Name . . . 6
   I.146.viii; II.336.iii; VI.306.iv, v
All kinds and all degrees of sin 22
   X.263
Amazing height of love Divine! 4
   II.338–9.vi; II.314.xvii–xix
   S i.*b*—We praise with all Thy hosts above
   S i.*d*—redeeming love
Among the dead in vain 112
   X.437
Ancient of Days, why didst Thou come . . . 9
   IV.343–4.iv, vi, vii, x
And shall I let Him go? 94
   III.276–7.1, ii, iv, v, vi, viii
Arise, all-seeing God, arise 95
   VIII.404–5.i, ix–xii
   S i.*a*—Arise, Thou jealous God
   S ii and iii—*Singular*
As my day my strength hath been . . . 79
   IX.113.N356; XIII.65.N3158; IX.120.N370
   S ii—*Second person* throughout
   S ii.*a*—Jesus, I from Thee receive
   S ii.*f*—nature's lusts fulfil
   S iii.*a*—By faith I on His strength
   S iii.*c*—Divinely confident
   S iii.*e*—I shall perform His
   S iii.*f*—And do the thing impossible
As taught by Thee, O God, I pray . . . 34
   X.83–4.i, vi–x
Author of every work divine 8
   IV.198–9. iv, vi
Author of my faith, I look 69
   XIII.41.i
   Plural throughout
Away with our fears 82
   XII.46–7.i.*abcd*, ii.*abcd*, iii.*efgh*
   S iii.*a*—With Jesus endure

Behold the mighty Prince of peace . . . 83
   III.139–40.xii, xiii, xv, xvii
   S i.*a*—It seals the universal peace
   S ii.*c*—and fix in every
Bewildered, lost, I must stand still . . . 19
   IX.215
   S ii.*b*—And make a worm

INDEX OF FIRST LINES AND SOURCES

Blessing, honour, thanks, and praise . . . 98
   II.188–9.i, iii, v
Blest be our everlasting Lord 3
   IX.204.N641, N642, N643

Celebrate Immanuel's name 105
   X.141–2
Christ for ever lives to pray 80
   XIII.136.ii
Christ, our Head and common Lord . . . 87
   II.224.i; 223.ii.*abcd*, iv.*efgh*
   S ii.*f*—Perfect him and us
   S ii.*h*—Thy only will
Christ, our living Head, draw near . . . 114
   IV.148–9.i, ii, iii, v, vii, viii
   S iv.*b*—All might see
Collected, perfected in one 134
   X.108–9
   S ii.*a*—O might I
Come, all who truly bear 90
   III.224–5
   S ii.*e*—dear peculiar ones
   S iv.*e*—The sheep of Israel's fold
   S iv.*f*—In *England's* pastures fed
Come, Father, Son, and Holy Ghost . . . 165
   VI.407–8.i, iii, iv, v
   S iii.*b*—Be here cut off
Come, gracious Lord, Thy counsel tell . . . 23
   XIII.11–12.ii.*efgh*, iii,iv.*abgh*
   S i.*a*—But let my Lord His counsel
   S i.*b*—sin in saints
   S ii.*a*—our inward parts
   S ii.*b*—our hearts
   S ii.*d*—Out of a foul
   S iv.*d*—reign in faithful hearts
Come, Holy Ghost, set to Thy seal . . . 90
   III.220–1.i, ii, iv
   S ii.*b*—O that we now may be
   S ii.*d*—His Passion
Come let us arise 73
   V.320–1.i, ii, v, vi, ix, x
Come, let us join with one accord . . . 93
   III.283–4.i, ii.*abcdef*, iv.*abcdef*
   S i.*f*—wait to see our heavenly
   S ii.*b*—We soon with Him
Come, let us our good God proclaim . . . 169
   VI.446–8.N78.i, ii, viii; N76.vi
   S iii.*b*—we feebly join
Come let us rise with Christ our Head . . . 114
   XIII.85–6

INDEX OF FIRST LINES AND SOURCES

Come let us who in Christ believe . . . 98
   II.191
   S ii.*c*—shall raise him up
   S ii.*d*—the starry crown
   S iii.*cd*—And we shall
Come, O my Hope, my Life, my Lord . . . 31
   I.75–6.xvi, xvii
   S i.*a*—Come then
Come, O my Jesu, from above 157
   V.145–6.i, iii, iv, vi
   S i.*a*—Come then, my Jesu
   S i.*d*—Thou bleeding Saviour
Come, O my soul, the call obey 156
   V.141–52, N1.i; N5.i, iv, v
   S ii.*a*—On my Pattern
   S iii.*a*—O might it now
Come, O Thou Breath Divine 122
   X.61
   S ii.*f*—Throughout the earth
Come, O Thou greater than our heart . . . 68
   II.332.i, ii
Come, O Thou Prophet, Priest, and King . . 31
   V.325.xii, xiii
   S i.*f*—in Thy right
Come then to Thy creature, and tell . . . 21
   VII.318.iii
Come Wisdom, Power, and Grace divine . . 167
   VII.43–4.i, ii, v
Come, ye that seek the Lord 113
   IV.143–4.i, iii.*efgh*, iv.*efgh*
Conqueror of sin and hell and death . . . 84
   II.362.ix, x, xi

Darkness and clouds around me roll . . . 57
   IX.174
Do what Thou wilt; it should be so . . . 50
   XI.502
   S i.*e*—shall ere long unwind the maze
   S i.*g*—then I see

Every gospel-minister 141
   X.295–6.N408, N410
   S i.*cd*—Plural
   S i.*h*—Then our souls
   S ii.*b*—Unconcern'd for numbers I
   S ii.*cg*—my
Extended on a cursèd tree 36
   I.232–3.i–iv, vii

INDEX OF FIRST LINES AND SOURCES

Far from myself to Thee 14
   VII.102.iv
Father, God, we glorify 113
   IV.141–2
Father, if mine in Christ Thou art . . . 70
   XIII.98
Father, instruct my docile heart 164
   IX.94
Father of all, by whom we are 164
   VII.72.i
   S ii.*a*—Poor worms
Father of all, we worship Thee 120
   XIII.24.i; VII.310.i
Father of Jesus Christ, the Just 14
   IV.227–8.i, ii, iii, iv.*abcd*, v.*ef*
   S i.*e*—But only Thou
   S ii.*f*—And call my darkness
Father of Lights, from whom proceeds . . . 17
   I.76–9.i, ii, iii, iv.*ab*, v.*cdef*, vii, viii
Father of me, and all mankind 130
   XI.200.i, ii.*cdab*, iii.*efgh*, v
Father of our dear Lord 121
   III.98–9
   S i.*c*—Over all Thy works it shone
Father of uncreated light 1
   II.194–5.i, ii, iii, iv, vi
   S iii.*a*—clouds
Father, Son and Holy Ghost 89
   V.389.i.*abcd*, ii
   S ii.*c*—On her new-born
   S iii.*d*—in her heart
Father, Son, and Spirit, come 163
   VII.68.i
Father, Son, and Spirit, come 20
   VII.33–4
Father, Thou hast our hearts inclined . . . 12
   XI.386.i, ii
   S i.*d*—And cannot
   S i.*e*—Till Thou Thine
   S ii.*a*—To this
   S ii.*d*—Add us to Jesus'
   S ii.*f*—And fear gives
Father, Thy boundless love we find . . . 71
   XI.155
   S ii.*a*—O could I
Fly, sinners, fly to David's Son 38
   IX.161
Forth in Thy strength, O Lord, I go . . . 144
   I.239–40
   S i.*c*—Thy only righteousness

INDEX OF FIRST LINES AND SOURCES

From sin and misery 24
   XI.265–6.iii, iv
   S i.*b*—Come then

Gentle and meek He comes to those . . . 109
   X.338
   S ii.*b*—Thy kingdom open'd in
Giver of concord, Prince of peace . . . 125
   I.298–9.i, iv, vii, ix
Glorious God, accept a heart 7
   VI.381.i; VIII.17.vii
   S i.*b*—That pants
Glory, and thanks, and love 3
   VI.285–6.i, ii
   S ii.*g*—on the cloud
Glory be to God above 87
   II.220–1.i, ii.*efgh*, iii.*abcd*, v.*abcd*, vi.*efgh*
   S i.*h*—the bleeding Lamb
   S iii.*a*—Surely He will not
Glory be to God on high 99
   IV.221–2
   S iv.*b*—We shall from the vale
Glory, love, and praise, and honour . . . 161
   III.364.i
God, be mercifully near 167
   VIII.409
   S i.*b*—of my father's
God in mortal flesh revealed 104
   XIII.101
God, on us Thy grace bestow 131
   VIII.147–8
   S i—*Third person*
   S iv.*a*—Then to perfect
Grant my importunate request 76
   III.19.x.*abcd*; I.340.vi.*ef*, v
   S i.*e*—And, arm'd with Thy great Spirit's aid
   S ii.*b*—all our sins
   S ii.*c*—O form the Saviour in
   S ii.*e*—be His name impress'd
Grant that to Thee my constant mind . . . 52
   II.273.ix, x
   S i.*a*—O that to Thee
   S i.*b*—Might with
   S ii.*a*—O that my tender soul might
Great Author of my being 147
   VII.132.i
Great triune God, Thy servants own . . . 95
   X.442
Greater love is not in man 111
   XII.26

INDEX OF FIRST LINES AND SOURCES

Guardian of my hoary hairs 145	
VIII.430–1	

Hail, great Physician of mankind! . . . 151
   V.65–6
   S i.*b*—Jesus Thou art
   S i.*c*—in Thine only name
   S ii.*b*—the languid body
Hail, holy, heaven-descended Child . . . 107
   X.143
   S ii.*e*—Jesus, Thy prostrate
   S ii.*f*—I now present
Hail, holy martyrs, glorious names . . . 61
   I.345–6
   S xi.*d*—the starry crown
Happy might I stationed be 109
   X.427–8.i, ii.*efgh*
   S i.*c*—my suit admit
Happy the men who Jesus know . . . 64
   IX.393.i, ii, iii
   S ii.*c*—Might with Himself
Happy the souls that followed Thee . . . 93
   III.322–3.i, iii, v, vii
   S i.*b*—to the accursed wood
Happy who the angels' word 107
   XI.118
He is wrapped in swaddling bands . . . 105
   XI.115–16.i.*efgh*, ii
   S i.*a*—Wrapped Himself in
He lifts the hands, stretched out so late . . . 116
   XI.316
He visits us unsought 10
   XII.13
Head of the Church, appear, appear . . . 85
   VII.49
Head of Thy suffering Church below . . . 122
   IV.47–8.i, v, vii–x
   S—*Plural* throughout
   S i.*b*—We ask in faith the passive
   S i.*d*—arm us
   S ii.*b*—succours
   S v.*d*—the starry crown
   S vi.*b*—to the wood
   S vi.*d*—his soul to God
Help, Lord! the busy foe 147
   V.51–2
   S i.*c*—a standard
His arm the almighty Father bared . . . 66
   XI.111
   S iii—us potsherds of the earth

INDEX OF FIRST LINES AND SOURCES

Holy and true and righteous Lord . . .	35
II.322.xxiii–xxvi	
S ii.*c*—the meek	
Holy Child, of heavenly birth	170
VI.401.i, v, vi	
Holy Ghost, with grace inspire	50
XIII.65	
S i.*f*—That nature's will	
How long, Thou faithful God, shall I . . .	92
III.257.i, iv, vi	
How may we resemble God	70
X.172–3	
How shall a sinful man presume . . .	13
IX.317	
S i.*a*—sinful worm	
S iii.*f*—And smiling in	
Humbly prostrate at Thy feet	159
VII.97.vii, vi	
I know in whom I have believed . . .	81
XIII.105	
I know the power was Thine	51
IX.22.i	
I leave my cares and fears below . . .	47
X.162	
S i.*a*—I leave a careless world	
S i.*b*—Mix'd with the multitudes I go	
I thank Thee, Lord of earth and heaven . . .	139
V.96–103.N10.i, N6.ii, N7.ix, N9.i, ii	
I too, forewarned by Jesu's love	151
XIII.191	
S ii.*d*—Mine everlasting	
If death my friend and me divide . . .	161
XIII.91.i, ii	
If mercies without end could move . . .	21
IX.157–8	
If Thou preserve our souls in peace . . .	61
VI.105.iii; V.251.vii	
If Thou the power of faith impart . . .	71
X.171–2.iv, vii, viii	
S ii.*d*—Thy sweet forgiving	
S iii.*c*—And can like Thee	
In rapture lost, on Thee I gaze	76
III.33.ii.*a*; IX.335.i.*acdef*, ii	
Jesu, descend again	102
III.371.iii; I.338.x	
Jesu, great Shepherd of the sheep . . .	126
V.33–4.i, iii–v	

INDEX OF FIRST LINES AND SOURCES

Jesu, Lord, we look to Thee	168
V.52–3	
S i.*d*—our jars for ever	
S iv.*c*—To Thy church	
S v.*b*—in God abide	
Jesu, my great High-Priest above	45
I.187–8.i	
Jesu, my soul takes hold on Thee	82
II.313.xi	
Jesu, shall I never be	68
II.276–7.i.*ab*, ix.*cd*, ii, iii, vi	
Jesu, Shepherd of the sheep	52
IV.449–50	
Jesu, Thine aid afford	12
I.266–9.ii, iii, viii, xviii, xx	
Jesu, Thy legacy I take	155
V.152.i; X.397.ii; VI.135.N30	
S ii and iii—*Plural* throughout	
S ii.*a*—O could we with His	
S ii.*c*—Meek as our Lord	
Jesu, Thy weakest servant bless	91
III.249	
S i.*a*—servants	
Jesu, to whose supreme command	30
II.332.iii, iv, vi, vii	
Plural throughout	
S iii.*b*—the Father's favourite Son	
S iii.*c*—Thee our Great Head	
S iv.*b*—The Lord is King, Messiah reigns	
Jesu, we hang upon the word	118
IV.172–3.i.*abcd*, ii.*ef*, iii, iv, v	
S iii.*e*—Repeat the melancholy moan	
S iv.*cd*—O might	
Jesus, by faith approaching Thee	26
X.224	
Jesus, by pangs of death oppressed	110
IX.142.ii	
S i.*a*—He, by the pangs	
Jesus, from whom all blessings flow	142
V.481–3.i, v, vi, ix, xi	
S ii.*a*—Thither collect Thy	
S v.*d*—might I	
Jesus, I make Thy brethren mine	47
X.243–4.N267.*efgh*	
Jesus, in whom the Godhead's rays	29
I.260–1	
S i.*b*—with milder majesty	
Jesus, in earth and heaven the same	88
X.322	
S ii.*a*—To each	

INDEX OF FIRST LINES AND SOURCES

Jesus, life of the believer	74
XIII.91.ii, i	
S ii.*a*—fruit of Jesus' passion	
Jesus, my faithful Guide	148
VII.137–8.i, ii	
Jesus, my strength and righteousness . . .	138
IV.232.i.*abcd*, ii.*abcd*, iii.*abcd*	
Jesus, plant Thy Spirit in me	32
XIII.66	
Jesus, Son of God and man	68
XI.294	
Jesus, suffering Son of God	23
XIII.70–1	
Jesus, that new command of Thine . . .	71
XII.26	
S i.*a*—I languish	
Jesus, the crowning grace impart . . .	65
X.163	
Jesus, the grace re-give	51
X.258–9	
Jesus the just, the good	152
VII.361–2.i.*abcd*, ii.*abcd*, iii	
Jesus, Thee the Head we own	126
XII.57	
S i.*d*—Hast *Jews* and *Gentiles* join'd	
Jesus, Thou art the Lord most high . . .	32
XIII.94.i.*efgh*, ii.*abcd*, iii, iv	
S ii.*g*—And good brought out of	
S iii.*g*—As mix'd	
Jesus, Thou dost not sue in vain . . .	39
IX.101	
S i.*c*—Thyself hast placed	
S i.*e*—While knocking	
S i.*f*—And criest 'My son'	
S ii.*a*—Supplicant	
Jesus, Thou say'st I shall receive . . .	33
XI.47–8.i, ii, iii.*efgh*, iv.*abcd*	
S iii.*b*—The root shall be	
S iii.*e*—I need	
S iii.*g*—I pant	
Jesus, Thy servants bless	138
XII.456	
Jesus, Thy weakest followers here . . .	117
XII.12–13.i, ii, iv	
Jesus, we wait to see	134
IX.471	
S ii.*c*—with time, obtain	
S ii.*f*—The whole of human race	
Jesus, with Thy Father come	128
XII.58–9.i, ii	

INDEX OF FIRST LINES AND SOURCES

Lamb of God, we follow Thee	63
IV.34–5.i, ii, iii, v, vii, viii	
Let all who speak in Jesu's name	137
XIII.183	
Let heaven and earth agree	120
III.347	
Let the world their virtue boast	54
II.317–19.i–v, vii–ix	
Let us triumphantly ride on	102
I.315.xxxiii, xxxv, xxxvi	
Lift up your heads, ye gates	115
IV.153–4	
Lord, give me that pacific mind	70
X.163	
Lord, I believe Thy mercy's power	52
IX.94	
Lord, I despair myself to heal	27
I.82–3.iii–vi	
Lord, may I put Thy nature on	72
X.171.ii.*cdef*; XIII.92–3.ii.*abcd*, i, iii	
S i.*a*—So shall I put His bowels on	
S i.*b*—Who hellish hate by love o'ercame	
S i.*c*—Who made His murderers His care	
S i.*d*—O might I	
S iii.*e*—every soul expend	
S iii.*g*—The rival of	
Lord of all, with pure intent	88
XI.119–20	
Lord of souls He truly was	47
XI.286	
Lord, our life of faith and prayer	102
XI.177–8	
S ii.*g*—Thy bosom fly	
Lord, that every moment I	110
XIII.153–4.ii–vi	
S i.*a*—But that every	
Lord, that I may the doctrine know	63
XI.402.i, ii	
Lovely, meek, and gentle Lamb	65
X.260.i; II.79–80.v, vi.*efgh*; X.255.N293.*cdef*	
S i.*a*—Thou lovely	
S i.*b*—of pure humility	
S i.*c*—Call'd after Thy	
S i.*d*—And fain I would	
S ii.*a*—O the strength	
S ii.*b*—vanity subdue	
S v.*a*—In Thy gentleness of mind	
Make our earthly souls a field	129
X.55.N1386.i; N1385	

INDEX OF FIRST LINES AND SOURCES

S i.*f*—Thy praise may show
S ii.*a*—Us who climb Thy holy hill
S ii.*b*—A general blessing make
May I, may all who humbly wait . . . 78
   II.242–4.xxii, iii, v, vi, viii, xi, xxiii
   S i.*b*—The glorious
   S ii.*b*—His promised aid
   S iii.*d*—My soul on Christ
   S iv.*b*—My Jesus shall subdue
   S iv.*c*—His healing
   S v.*b*—The promise
   S v.*cd*—*Third person*
Me when an enemy to God 156
   X.318.iii, ii
   S ii—I could
Meanest of all who Thee confess . . . 139
   V.483.xii, xiii, xiv
   S i.*a*—O might my lot be cast with these
   S i.*b*—of Jesu's witnesses
   S i.*c*—that my Lord would count me
   S i.*d*—His dear
   S ii.*a*—This only thing
Meet and right it is that all 5
   XII.144.i.*efgh*, ii
   S ii.*c*—God descended
   S ii.*d*—By Thy blood
Monarch of all, with lowly fear 41
   I.104–5.i, iii–viii
   S vii.*c*—we raise
More than a host of angels 149
   XII.439.ii.*fghij*
Most gracious Lord 37
   XIII.81–2.i, iii, iv, v
Most meek and tender-hearted Lamb . . . 160
   V.74–5.i, ii, iii, iv.*abc*, vi.*abc*
   S i.*f*—For God-with-us is man
   S iii.*b*—favourite
   S iv.*c*—In all things let him be
My Father, O my Father, hear 49
   II.203–6.i–vi
   S vii—*Editor*
My health, my light, my life, my crown . . . 15
   I.140.x, xii; XI.121.iii
   S iii.*b*—On a proud abject worm
My heavenly Lord, I would from Thee . . . 137
   XI.161.ii
My mortal foe, whom for Thy sake . . . 156
   X.172
My pattern in Thy death I see 158
   V.147–50.N4.vi; N7.v.*abc*, iv.*def*; N6.vi

INDEX OF FIRST LINES AND SOURCES

S i.*a*—here I plainly see
S ii.*a*—for Jesus lost
S ii.*b*—found in God
S ii.*e*—And who for Thee
S iii.*c*—Here let me ever, ever stay

No, Lord, it cannot shortened be . . . 77
   IX.69–70
   S i.*b*—which plagued the '*Egyptian* race
No, they cry, it cannot be 125
   X.42–3
Not in the strong impetuous wind . . . 16
   IX.180–1.N566, N568, iii.*efgh*
   S i.*d*—Which rents
   S iii.*a*—I pant
Not with these eyes of flesh and blood . . . 48
   XI.321–2.iii, iv

O all-atoning Lamb 140
   III.78–9.i, ii, iii, vii, iv, v.*abcd*, vi.*efgh*
   S iii.*d*—fervent charity
   S vi.*e*—I rise at Thy command
O God, at Thy command we rise . . . 2
   IX.225, N706; I.299.i
O God, forgivenesses are Thine 78
   IV.4.viii
   S i.*a*—But O, forgivenesses
O God of my salvation, hear 45
   II.233–4.i, ii, xiii.*abc*, xiv.*ab*, xiii.*f*, xvii, xviii
   S i.*e*—smile to see me feebly bring
   S v.*b*—and take me home
O God of truth and love 92
   III.252–3
   S ii.*a*—O might
O Jesus, let Thy dying cry 111
   X.430–1
O Lord, our strength and righteousness . . . 96
   VI.99–100.i, ii, v
   S iii.*a*—Wherefore to Thine
O most compassionate High-priest . . . 97
   VI.118.i, ii, iv
   S—*Third person* throughout
   S i.*a*—Ah! most compassionate
   S iii.*f*—And prop them with
O Son of God, in vain 26
   XIII.201–2.i.*abcd*, ii.*abcd*, iii.*abcd*, iv, v
O that the power were mine 44
   XIII.177.i, ii
O Thou Good Samaritan 12
   II.157.vi
   S i.*h*—Who gasp

INDEX OF FIRST LINES AND SOURCES

O Thou who hast the victory won . . . 51
   XIII.232.iii
O Thou, whose word is life and power . . . 53
   XI.367–8, N1720.*abcd*; N1722.iii.*abcd*, iv.*abcd*
   S i.*a*—The Man whose
   S i.*c*—Who only could
Obedient to our Lord's command . . . 124
   XII.28–9
   S iii.*e*—And to Thy church
Of all our bliss the fount and root . . . 152
   VII.103.iii.*defabc*, iv; IV.317.vi
   S i.*df*—*Third person*
   S i.*e*—Heaven its
   S ii.*b*—Glorious earnest
   S iii.*a*—Then, Saviour, then my soul receive
   S iii.*b*—Transported from the vale
Oh let me of Thy strength take hold . . . 67
   II.350.xi; XIII.129.ii.*abcd*
   S i.*a*—O let us
Oh let Thy death's mysterious power . . . 111
   X.431.iii
Oh may I, like Jesus, be 75
   XII.71
   S i.*a*—O might I
Oh may I tempt my God no more . . . 66
   X.154
   S i.*b*—Or wantonly
Oh that Thou wouldst the heavens rent . . . 30
   I.269–71.i, iv, vi, vii
Oh who can of Thy grace despair . . . 23
   XII.97.iii, iv, vi
   S ii.*d*—my gasping spirit
One God the children all confess . . . 133
   XI.460–1.ii–v
   S ii.*a*—Yet millions still uncall'd
Our friendship sanctify and guide . . . 162
   V.409–10.ii, iii, iv.*abcdef*, v.*abcjkl*
   S i.*d*—our intercourse
   S i.*f*—And never meet but in Thy
   S vi.*c*—Thou know'st, dear Lord, what we would say
Our Jesus is gone up on high 82
   V.318–20.ii–vii, xviii
   S vi.*b*—Till we His image
   S vi.*c*—Experiencing His
   S vi.*d*—And brought
   S vii.*b*—The whole doth
   S vii.*d*—And perfectly

INDEX OF FIRST LINES AND SOURCES

Our King we now go forth to meet . . . 108
   XI.485–6.i.*ab*, iii.*ab*, iv, v, vi
   S i.*a*—The people still go
Our privilege to deal 97
   XII.197.i.*efgh*, ii.*efgh*, iii
   S—*Third person* throughout
   S i.*c*—with the meat
   S i.*f*—His people multiply
   S ii.*e*—Make the full proof
   S ii.*f*—On multitudes
   S ii.*gh*—Go on to

Peace be on this house bestowed . . . 159
   II.219.i, ii
Physician, Friend of human kind . . . 136
   V.391–2.i, v
   S ii.*a*—in that name
Physician of the sin-sick race 27
   X.43–4
Plant, and root, and fix in me 75
   II.277–8.x, xii, xiv, xv, xvi, xvii, xx
   S v.*b*—I shall have no power to sin
Plant in me Thy constant mind . . . 69
   VI.404.vii; XIII.222.ii.*acbd*
   S i—*Plural* throughout
Poor and ignorant and blind 19
   XII.236
   S ii.*g*—Then I feel the
   S ii.*h*—Then I know
Prince and Saviour of mankind 22
   XI.356–7
Prisoner of hope, I wait the hour . . . 28
   II.140–1.vi–xi

Quickened with our immortal Head . . . 80
   XIII.104
   S i.*g*—And all Thy saints

Rejoice in Jesu's birth 106
   IX.381–2.N1080.i.*abcd*, N1081.i, ii
Rejoice, rejoice, ye fallen race 117
   II.227.i, ii, 252.xii
   S iii.*a*—O the grace
   S iii.*b*—While eternal
   S iii.*c*—God delights
   S iii.*d*—Soul of each
Rejoice, ye followers of your Lord . . . 137
   XI.297
Repentance upon both bestow 158
   VI.186.x

INDEX OF FIRST LINES AND SOURCES

Rest to my soul I long to find 59
   XIII.125–6
   S i.*a*—I gasp to find
   S ii.*a*—Thy feeblest servant

Salvation to our God 6
   III.336.iii.*efgh*, iv
Saviour and Friend of men 85
   XII.285.ii, iii, i
   S ii.*def*—*Editor*
   S iii.*cd*—*Editor*
   S iii.*f*—And with our open'd hearts
Saviour, I joyfully agree 164
   XI.30–1.i, ii, iii, v
   S i.*a*—I yield, I joyfully agree
   S iii.*a*—Thine hand
Saviour, I know Thy gracious will . . . 41
   XIII.231.i, iii
   S ii.*c*—O wouldst Thou
   S ii.*f*—And on
Saviour of all, to Thee we bow 40
   II.361.i, ii
Saviour of my soul from sin 43
   III.249–50
   S i.*c*—dost begin
Saviour, the mystery of Thy grace . . . 6
   XI.302.ii
Saviour, Thy flesh is meat indeed . . . 89
   XI.390.N1778, N1779.*efgh*, N1780.*abcd*
   S ii—*Singular* throughout
   S ii.*a*—But sure
   S ii.*g*—a pilgrim
Searcher of hearts, to Thee I fly 170
   VII.151–2.i, ii.*ab*, iii.*cdef*, iv–vi
   S i.*e*—my partner's heart
   S ii.*c*—Without Thy grace he lives
   S ii.*d*—of death and judgment near
   S iii.*d*—Ah, give him
   S v.*a*—O might we
See, gracious Lord, with pitying eyes . . . 159
   II.216
   S i.*b*—Beneath Thy hand a sufferer lies
   S i.*c*—Thy mercy not Thine anger proves
   S i.*d*—And sick he is whom Jesus loves
   S vi.*d*—And glorious all, and
See, the Desire of Nations comes . . . 10
   I.78–81.ii, iii.*abcd*, iv.*abcd*, v.*abcd*, xi
   S i.*b*—Nor outward
   S v.*a*—But, O
   S vi.*a*—His numerous seed He now shall see

INDEX OF FIRST LINES AND SOURCES

Servant of God and Son of Man 132
    IX.413–15.N1146.i, N1149.i, iii
    S iii.*a*—O might it now from Thee
Shepherd of souls, the great, the good . . . 143
    VI.107–8.i, ii, v–ix
    S i.*d*—sheep of *England's* fold
    S iii.*f*—Can land them
    S iv.*f*—To chase both
Shepherds the sheep should feed 136
    XI.180
    S i.*a*—Pastors the sheep
    S i.*h*—Whate'er the 'Almighty can
Sinful and blind and poor 17
    III.265
Sing we merrily to God 2
    IX.312
Sing with glad anticipation 101
    XIII.238; 218.i, iii, iv
    S ii.*d*—While He pompously
    S iv.*e*—Now assume it
Sing, ye happy souls, that press 86
    X.37
Sion, rejoice thy King to see 108
    XI.486–7.ii.*badcef*, iii
Sleep that soothingly restores 166
    VII.128–9.i–iv, vi
    S ii.*d*—the balmy blessing
Sons of God, triumphant rise 95
    I.170.i, ii, iii
Soon as I find myself forsook 52
    II.202.vii
Sorrow may enter and remain 172
    XII.37.ii
Sovereign, universal King 15
    X.140.iii
    S i.*h*—Reign in every
Spirit of faith come down on me . . . 30
    IX.138–9
Spirit of interceding grace 44
    XIII.13–14
Still let Thy wisdom be my guide . . . 42
    I.89–90.v, vi
Still on the soul of fallen man 8
    XI.319
    S ii.*c*—Or knows
    S ii.*d*—Or feels
Still the Holy Ghost descends 119
    XII.358.ii, iii
    S ii.*b*—This gospel truth to seal

INDEX OF FIRST LINES AND SOURCES

Straitened in God we cannot be 77
    IX.190.N597.i.*abcd*, ii.*abcd*, N589.i.*abcd*
    S iii.*d*—And when we grace
Stupendous love of God Most High! . . . 11
    X.253–4.i, v, vi
Sun of righteousness, arise 14
    X.134
    S i.*e*—Chase the darkness of

Thankful for our every blessing 162
    III.367
Thanks be to God who gave 121
    VI.286–7. v, vi
That mighty faith on me bestow . . . 67
    X.293
That steadfast faith divine 67
    XIII.112–13
    S i.*e*—In every time
The children in their earliest days . . . 165
    VI.452
    S ii–iv—*First person* throughout
    S ii.*a*—One of those happy children, me
    S ii.*b*—Saviour into
    S iii.*a*—They tell me Thou
Thee the angelic armies praise 5
    IX.226
The first faint spark of good desire . . . 80
    X.116
    S ii.*b*—shine into
The God of all grace 119
    XII.167–8.i, ii, iv
    S i.*d*—And sent Him
The holy Jesus rests in hope 111
    XII.99.i, ii, iii
    S iii.*a*—O might I
    S iii.*b*—Meekly to God my soul
    S iii.*c*—Into my Father's hands
The honour we claim 48
    III.365.i.*def*, ii.*def*
The Lamb from the throne 103
    VII.81.iii; IV.133.iii; VII.81.v.*abc*; IV.122–3.v, vi,
        ix, x, vii, viii
    S iii.*a*—He comes
    S iii.*c*—vouchsafes
    S ix.*a*—On Jesus's face
    S ix.*c*—pleasures ecstatic, the cherubim gaze
    S x.*ab*—*Third person*
The Lord of life is risen indeed 112
    IV.130.ix–xi

INDEX OF FIRST LINES AND SOURCES

The living principle of grace 81
   XIII.212
The love impartial and sincere 123
   XI.511–12
   S i, ii, iii.*b*—*Singular*
   S i.*d*—could find
   S iv.*f*—these Christians live
The Name be known from east to west . . . 130
   X.128
The solemn hour is come 107
   XIII.257.i, iii
The Spirit of our Head 118
   XI.181.ii, iii
The table of my heart prepare 64
   IX.94
The work of faith with heaven begun . . . 57
   XIII.89–90.i, iii–v
   S iii.*a*—But O Thou patient mournful Man
   S iii.*b*—Thy life our better way we
   S iv.*c*—And suffer till our final groan
The world's bright Day did then appear . . . 129
   XI.439.i–iii
   S iii.*c*—The beams of glory dart
   S iii.*d*—Our sin
   S iii.*e*—cheer our
This is His good and perfect will . . . 74
   V.319.x; XIII.40.ii
   S i.*a*—His acceptable will
   S ii.*c*—And on we to
This pain, this consecrated pain 150
   XIII.158–9.iii
   S—*Third person* throughout
Thou art Thyself the seal 78
   I.101.viii
Thou canst not, Lord, a beggar spurn . . . 38
   IX.143–4.N443, N444.*abcd*, N445.*abcd*, N446.*abcd*
   S iii.*a*—by the world abhorr'd
Thou God of harmony and love . . . 135
   IV.243–4.i, ii, v, vii
   S i.*f*—The heavenly
   S iv.*a*—O might I
   S iv.*e*—heavenly harper
Thou goest about in every age 9
   X.229
Thou Lamb of God, Thou Prince of peace . . 150
   I.129
Thou, Lord, hast given the wish to pray . . . 43
   V.174–6.iii, vi–viii
   Plural throughout

INDEX OF FIRST LINES AND SOURCES

    S i.*a*—Proceeds from Thee the wish
    S iv.*a*—regard the joint complaint
    S iv.*b*—Of all Thy tempted
    S iv.*c*—supply the common want
Thou, my most condescending Lord .   .   . 37
    IX.101
    S i.*a*—O my most condescending
    S i.*b*—He humbly stoops
    S i.*e*—*Third person*
    S ii.*d*—Whate'er my Lord commands
    S ii.*e*—all my Saviour's will
    S ii.*f*—His law
Thou out of great distress 100
    V.221.vii, viii, x
Thou promisest Thyself to impart .   .   . 35
    XI.356
Thy call, O God, to man conveys .   .   . 142
    IX.156
Thy will, O Lord, whate'er I do .   .   . 38
    X.204–5.ii
Till Thou anew my soul create 21
    II.273.xi–xiv
'Tis finished! The Messiah dies 109
    XII.99–100.i, iii, v
'Tis not enough for me to know .   .   . 48
    XI.363
To us the new command He gives .   .   . 124
    XII.96.iii, iv, vi
To what am I reserved? Great God .   .   . 148
    VII.180–1.i–iii, viii
Today, while it is called today 18
    XIII.122–3.i.*abcd*, ii.*efgh*, iii
    S iv.*b*—I am not fit for Thee
    S iv.*c*—Yet trust
Triumphant soul, the hour is come .   .   . 171
    II.173–6.N3.i, ii; N4.iii, iv, viii, ix
    S iii.*a*—dying saint
    S iii.*e*—mouldering clod
    S vi.*e*—And I shall
    S vi.*f*—And I shall meet my sister
True Light of the whole world, appear .   .   . 11
    XI.319–20
    S i.*f*—To that
    S iii.*d*—Let man
    S iii.*e*—offerest once
Turn, O Thou good Physician, turn .   .   . 28
    X.225.i.*abcd*, ii.*ef*
    S i.*a*—Turn then
    S i.*e*—And lo

INDEX OF FIRST LINES AND SOURCES

Unchangeable, Almighty Lord 127
   II.333–4.i, ii, v, vi, viii, ix
Unnumbered deaths and snares 153
   VII.392–3.v, vi, viii

Vanquished by injurious ill 73
   XIII.19–20

Warned from the body to depart . . . 153
   VII.404
Weary of all this wordly strife 40
   VI.71–2.i, ii, v
What depths of wisdom and of grace . . . 11
   XIII.116.i, iii.*abcd*, ii.*efgh*
   S ii.*eh*—*Third person*
What endless scenes of wonder rise . . . 5
   XI.22
   S i.*c*—When Jesus face to face we see
   S i.*d*—His pomp and majesty
When, dearest Lord, when shall it be . . . 20
   II.258–9.i, ii, xii, xiii
When from flesh the spirit freed 99
   II.190.iii.*efgh*, iv
When He could Himself defend 154
   XII.81
When Jesus darts His glorious light . . . 6
   VI.455–6
When shall mine eyes behold the Lamb . . 24
   II.144–6.ii, x, iv, v, vi, vii, viii, xii, xiii, xiv
Whether the word be preached or read . . . 46
   XIII.123–5.i, ii, v, vi
   S ii.*b*—light to me
   S ii.*c*—darker still the dark it leaves
Who is this condescending Friend . . . 169
   XI.32
Whoe'er by Thy good Spirit are led . . . 35
   XIII.12
   S ii.*b*—my panting heart
With lowly reverential joy 149
   VI.167–8.iii, iv, vi
Witness, thou righteous man 58
   XIII.184–6.i, ii.*abcd*, iii.*ef*, iv, vi, viii, x, xi
   S i.*e*—Didst thou not knock
   S ii.*b*—Didst thou not seek
   S ii.*e*—Or didst thou toil
   S iii.*a*—When the old Adam was
   S v.*e*—Thy soul perspired
   S vii.*c*—And when

INDEX OF FIRST LINES AND SOURCES

Wretched in myself, I would 16
   X.254–5.i, ii.*efgh*, iii.*efgh*, iv.*efgh*

Ye kingdoms of the earth, arise 132
   VIII.153–4.xxvii, xxviii, xxx
Young men and maidens, raise 1
   VI.433–4
   S iii.*b*—excellences